MORE NEEDLEWORK
BLOCKING AND FINISHING

MORE NEEDLEWORK BLOCKING AND FINISHING

Dorothy Burchette

CHARLES SCRIBNER'S SONS / NEW YORK

Copyright © 1979 Dorothy Burchette

Library of Congress Cataloging in Publication Data

Burchette, Dorothy.
    More needlework blocking and finishing.

    1. Canvas embroidery.   I. Title.
TT778.C3B86   746.4′4   78-31607
ISBN 0-684-16147-8

1 3 5 7 9 11 13 15 17 19 M/C 20 18 16 14 12 10 8 6 4 2

Printed in the United States of America

Acknowledgments and Credits

Particular thanks to my husband, Bob, for his patience when his meals were late, and for never telling me, at 3 A.M., to turn the light off in the workroom. My editor, Elinor Parker, was more than understanding when the manuscript was late.

So many talented friends helped with designs and needlepoint. Many thanks to Gloria Archer, Mae Byers, Roswtha Colton, Betsy Edgeworth, Vivian Frisch, Ava Harrison, Chris Meyerhoff, Agnes Sanford, and Janet Sturtevant.

I won't forget the many men and women who have attended workshops the past few years. Their expressed need to know more led to this book.

PHOTOGRAPHY: Bob Burchette

NEEDLEWORK: Mrs. G. A. Archer—
Bell, Book, and Candle
Bookmark; Lunch
Box; Tea Cozy.
Mrs. Robert Byers—
Christmas Tree
Ornaments.
Mrs. Ava Harrison—
Bench Pad.
Mrs. F. LaMotte III—
Rug.

PATTERNS: Lee Harrison

NEEDLEWORK: Mrs. Chris Meyerhoff—
Speaker Cover.
Mrs. Thomas Offutt—
Card Table Cover.
Mrs. Agnes Sanford—
Needlework Case;
Overnight Bag;
Umbrella Cover.
Mrs. Jack White—
Tote Bag.

Contents

A Word with You   ix

SECTION I: KNOW HOW TO   1
Plan   2
Make a Pattern   6
Block   8
Glue   12
Sew   14
Care For It and Repair It   17

SECTION II: FEMININE AND FUN   23
Briefcase   24
Evening Bag   30
Lunch Box   33
Needlework Case   37
Overnight Bag   43
Paperweight   51
Pet Bed   53
Sleep Mask   58
Take-Along   61
Tennis Racquet Cover   66·
Tote Bag   70
Umbrella Cover   74

SECTION III: FOR MEN   79

Bookends   80

Bottle Carrier   84

Cummerbund   89

Desk Blotter—Covered Ends   91

Hatband   93

Letter Holder   95

Pencil Cup   98

Tobacco Pouches   100

SECTION IV: AROUND THE HOUSE   103

Bench Pad   104

Bookmark I   107

Bookmark II   109

Card Table Cover   110

Christmas Tree Ornaments   113

Desk Blotter—Covered Corners   115

Folding Chair   118

Padded Picture   122

Picture Frame   127

Speaker Cover   132

Tea Cozy   134

Yellow Pad Cover   138

RECOMMENDED PRODUCTS   143

NEEDLEWORK SOURCES   145

A Word with You

Some of us just don't know when to quit; so it is with needlepoint addicts. I've been one for many years. I know dozens of fellow needlepointers who occasionally let their families starve a little, overlook housework, and stay up half the night to do "just one more row."

Don't you think we have made enough pillows and pictures?

Here are some other items to intrigue you for a while, with instructions to produce them. These are all professional tricks used in the better shops. Throughout the book are suitable substitutes for equipment and findings available only to the trade. For instance, a good shop has a power machine with top and bottom feed, but a home sewing machine is fine if you use it to your advantage.

Remember, your valuable time went into working the needlepoint, and perhaps you designed it too. Don't you want the most professional results in finishing—without spending a small fortune?

The fundamentals are here to finish just about anything. Be imaginative and apply the methods to projects of your own—and have fun.

MORE NEEDLEWORK
BLOCKING AND FINISHING

SECTION I

KNOW HOW TO

Plan

Most designers of purchased painted designs or kits give little consideration to finishing. A thought about some of the following should influence your decision about buying or designing your own.

Decide the intended function of the article you plan to make. Ask yourself if there is enough extra canvas around the design to make blocking and finishing easy. What kind of lining or interlining is needed? Can the lining match or contrast? How about zippers or ribbon? Will it be machine- or hand-sewn? Will the needlepoint be movable, as on a cushion, or immovable, as in a picture frame? Where will you use it? All of these things tell you what allowances have to be made for finishing, where seams should be, what materials you need, and which stitches should be used. Some stitches distort the canvas if the needlepoint is to be movable. Watch out for these.

Once you know what is required, you can proceed. Make your pattern, if needed, and purchase the necessary items. It's easier to select lining fabrics or findings first and coordinate the needlepoint yarns to these. You can run yourself ragged going from store to store trying to match a certain color of yarn when what you have in mind may not be available.

Figure your approximate needs and purchase just a little bit more. By the time you are ready to use these materials, you may not be able to find more if you need it. Remember, it will take a while to finish the needlepoint.

SUGGESTED FABRICS FOR LININGS

CANVAS:
  You can make clean, sharp creases.
  It's hard wearing.
  It's heavy and firm.
  It requires a fabric protector spray.
  It's not available in too many colors.

ULTRASUEDE:

Edges can be left raw to eliminate bulk.

It's firm.

You can dry-clean it or wash it.

It's available in many colors.

It's elegant and expensive.

Needles and pins leave holes.

VELVETEEN:

It has a firm weave.

It's elegant for pictures and cushions.

It wears fairly well.

It's dry-cleanable.

It has to be steamed, not ironed.

MOIRE:

It has a firm, even weave.

It's lightweight.

Upholsterer's weight is available in many colors.

It's thick enough so glue won't show through.

It's dry-cleanable.

LEATHER:

It wears well.

It's very easy to glue.

It's luxurious.

It's hard to find in more than basic colors.

Pins and needles leave holes.

SILK:

It's usually a firm-weave fabric.

It's elegant.

It comes in many colors and weights.

Medium and light weights are good with spray adhesives.

It's dry-cleanable.

It water-spots.

SUEDE CLOTH (PLASTIC-COATED):

It has a firm weave.

You can leave raw edges or finish them off.

The color selection is good.

It's usually waterproof.

It's dry-cleanable.

Pins and needles leave holes on some.

SUGGESTED FABRICS FOR INTERLININGS

CANVAS:

It's firm and flexible.

PERMACRIN:

It's firmer, flexible, and plastic-coated.

PERMETTE CORNICE FABRIC:

It's very firm, of heavy weight, and not too flexible.

It's plastic-coated.

Do not sew it. Use masking tape.

MAT BOARD:

It's firm cardboard.

It's available in regular or double weight.

You can't sew it.

FOAM CORE BOARD:

It's ¼-inch-thick, stiff foam covered with paper.

It's featherweight.
It will not warp.
It's easy to cut.

TIPS ...

Keep the following things in mind when you are planning:

Add a few extra rows of tent stitch around needlepoint that is to be machine-stitched.

Cylindrical objects, such as the pencil cup, should be planned so the design continues at the seam (Photo 1).

1

If an item is to be worked in more than one piece and joined, the seams show less if they divide design areas (Photo 2).

Use needlepoint stitches that do not distort the canvas when the needlepoint is not permanently fixed to an unyielding surface. If you use a stitch that will pull the canvas out of shape too much, at least work the needlepoint on a frame.

If you intend to make an article without needlepointing the background (see "Speaker Cover" chapter, and Photo 198), don't worry about the canvas color. Pin the blank canvas to your blocking board over several sheets of newspaper. Pin as though you were blocking it. Spray it with any color waterproof paint you want. Allow it to dry on the board and then put your design on the canvas.

You usually need one extra row of needlepoint on any edge that is to be turned under. This extra row is pressed so it is right on the side, not top, of the edge. You don't want to see any unworked canvas or have your needlepoint too small if size is critical.

If you want to cut mat board and foam core board yourself, particularly beveled edges, invest in the mat cutter suggested in "Recommended Products."

2

Make a Pattern

TISSUE PATTERNS

1. Fit tissue paper on the article.
2. Fold out the surplus and Scotch-tape the folds.
3. Mark outside edges (Photo 3).
4. Trace the flattened pattern.
5. Allow seams, if needed.
6. Retrace for final pattern. Use black felt-tipped pen (Photo 4).
7. Trace onto needlepoint canvas.

MEASURED PATTERNS

1. If you have to pad an article yourself, glue on the padding first.
2. Measure and mark your dimensions on tracing paper. Use a black felt-tipped pen. Add seam allowances, if any.
3. Lay your blank canvas over this tracing and put the outlines on the canvas.

Use the same ruler or tape measure to take all measurements throughout a project. You would be surprised at the variance between different measuring devices.

Remember to allow the few extra rows needed to cover completely. For instance, the outside dimensions of the pencil cup were exactly 9 inches around by 3¾ inches high. You have to allow for the thickness of the ribbon and its seams plus the thickness of the needlepoint and its turned-under seams. You also have to add an additional row of needlepoint to the top and bottom. You will press the unworked canvas under and these extra rows will hide the bare canvas on the edge. The actual outside dimensions of the pencil cup, when finished, were 10 inches around by 3⅞ inches high.

You cannot always predict exactly how many rows you will need. It's a good idea to allow several inches of unworked canvas around the needlepoint in case you need to add extra rows after the needlepoint is blocked.

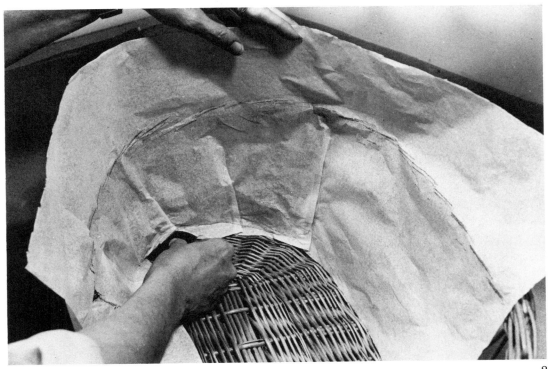

3

4

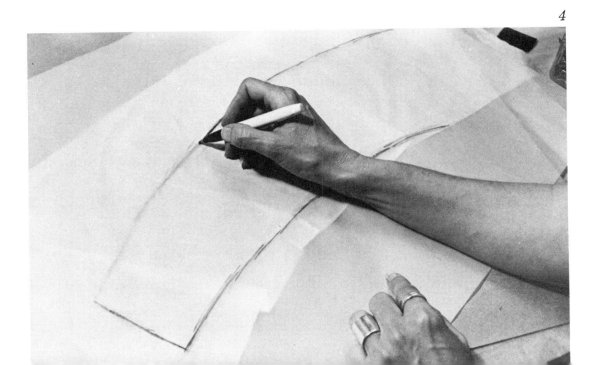

Block

EQUIPMENT

BLOCKING BOARD:

This can be a bulletin board, a ceiling tile, or a piece of "white board," available from your local building supply house. It is firm, but pins are inserted and removed easily. Spray it with acrylic before you use it, so it won't absorb moisture or stains.

STAINLESS-STEEL "T" PINS:

These are very easy to use and are rustproof. Rust will eat holes in canvas and yarns.

PORTABLE STEAMER:

I find the Oster Steam Wand the best. It can be held in any position and fits into tight areas for the final steaming. Don't go out and buy one if you have either of the other two listed in "Recommended Products." They work almost as well. You have to place your needlepoint in a horizontal position to use them. I find most steam irons just don't give enough steam. In a pinch, you can lay a clean, damp cloth over the wrong side of the needlepoint and create steam with a hot iron. Don't put the weight of the iron on the needlepoint.

PLASTIC TRIANGLE:

Use this as a guide for straight edges and square corners.

NORMAL BLOCKING

Block all pieces facedown unless they have raised stitches. Bleeding paints or dyes will show on the side that is exposed to the air. All moisture evaporates from this surface. Colors are carried with it and are drawn to the upper surface.

One of the advantages of using steam is that it does not remove from the canvas any of the sizing put there to help it retain its shape. Needlepoint dries so quickly after steaming that you don't waste a lot of time. It doesn't have a chance to mildew, and the possibility of bleeding colors is less.

Clip the selvage, if there is one, at 1-inch intervals. Place your needlepoint on the blocking board, facedown. Straighten one edge and begin placing pins in this edge. Square the corner with the plastic triangle and place pins down this second side. Apply steam all over the needlepoint and continue to square the remaining corners and straighten sides. You will have to apply more steam as you go, so that the canvas and yarn will give as you block. Insert pins about ½ inch apart on all sides and give the needlepoint and unworked canvas a final steaming (Photo 5).

STUBBORN PIECES

Needlepoint pieces that are badly out of shape may need more moisture than a steamer is capable of supplying. You can wrap the needlepoint in a damp cloth. Cover it with a piece of plastic or foil. Leave it overnight or until it absorbs enough moisture from the cloth. Make sure the cloth has not been washed in chlorine, as this will have a detrimental effect on the yarn dyes.

Another method is to spray the back of the needlepoint with a fine mist of water. Cover it and leave overnight. Either of these two methods increases the possibility of bleeding paints or

5

dyes, but you won't be removing any of the sizing.

METALLIC OR SILK FABRICS

Try to work these pieces on a needlepoint frame, so they will need minimal blocking. Stitches that do not distort the canvas are an advantage. Block facedown and use steam. If the metallic thread is synthetic, spray with a fine mist instead of steam. Heat will melt most synthetics.

SOILED NEEDLEPOINT

Occasionally a needlepoint piece will become soiled during working. I prefer having it dry-cleaned. This will not remove all of the sizing, as it is water-soluble. Ask your cleaner to clean it in new fluid and not to press it, steam it, or otherwise fool around with it. You probably know more about needlepoint than he does.

You can wash a soiled piece if you have to. Follow the directions in the chapter on "Care For It and Repair It." Block the damp needlepoint piece away from the sun or other source of heat. Size the back of it when it is almost dry and still pinned to the board.

SIZING

Perhaps you had to wash your needlepoint and that removed all the sizing, or perhaps you just want it firmer than it is. It's easy to resize it. Try one of the following formulas.

Rice has been used for centuries in the Orient for sizing embroidery and fine fabrics. It works on needlepoint too. It's very rich in starch and dries almost colorless. You won't be troubled with insects or objectionable odors as you would with an animal glue.

Have your needlepoint pinned to the blocking board, facedown. Paint the sizing on the back of the needlepoint with a pastry brush while still hot. Either formula can be diluted if you want a thinner sizing. Try not to force the sizing through the needlepoint to the right side, but just let it penetrate the threads on the back. Allow it to dry on the board.

FORMULA I
> ¼ cup *instant* rice
> ¼ cup water
> ½ cup warm water

Put rice into blender and grind as fine as possible. Combine powdered rice and ¼ cup water in a small pan. Bring to a boil. Let stand for a minute or two. Put ½ cup warm water into the blender and add the hot mixture. Blend until you have a smooth paste.

FORMULA II

¼ cup *natural* rice

¾ cup water

¼ cup warm water

Put rice in blender and grind as fine as possible. Combine powdered rice and ¾ cup water in a small pan. Bring to a boil and simmer, covered, until tender (about fifteen minutes). Put ¼ cup warm water in blender and add the rice mixture. Blend until you have a smooth paste.

TIPS . . .

Spray your painted canvas with a coat of acrylic before you work the needlepoint, so your paints won't run or bleed through the yarn during blocking.

Clip all loose threads from the back of the needlepoint. Do this as you work, to avoid a tiresome job and sore fingers.

Glue

EQUIPMENT

PRESSURE BOARDS:

Two pieces of ½-inch plywood. I find 16-inch-by-8-inch a good all-around size.

"C" CLAMPS:

Four clamps, 2- or 3-inch length.

SPRING CLAMPS:

Use these to apply pressure briefly on corners and small areas until you can put the item between the pressure boards.

WAXED PAPER:

It prevents the needlepoint from adhering to the pressure boards. Use it whenever you glue.

RUBBER BANDS:

Use these over a manila file folder or flexible cardboard to apply pressure to cylindrical objects (see "Pencil Cup" chapter and Photo 1).

CLOTHES PINS (CLAMP-TYPE):

Use these to apply pressure to top edges of cylindrical objects.

GLUE:

Tri-Tix Rubber Cream gets tacky quickly and dries fast. It rubs off tools and fingers easily and dries colorless and flexible.

Bond Instant Gr-r-rip doesn't get tacky as fast and is slightly slower drying. It dries colorless and flexible and washes off with water before it is dry.

Spray adhesive (there are several on the market) gets tacky quickly and dries fast. It is colorless and flexible. It makes possible even distribution on large surfaces. Remove with dry-cleaning fluid.

METHOD

Flat objects are spread with glue and placed between waxed paper and pressure boards. The boards are fastened

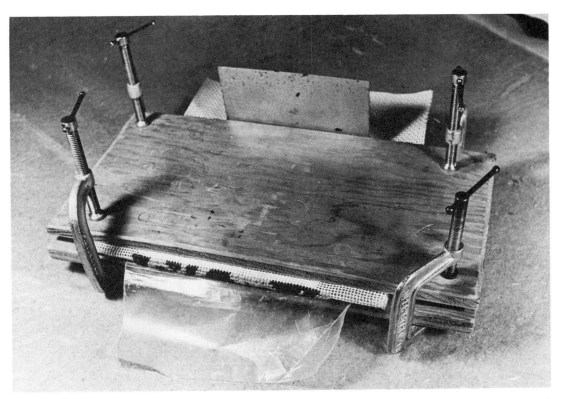

with "C" clamps at each corner (Photo 6).

Always apply an adhesive right up to the last row of needlepoint if a piece is to be cut close. It's very difficult to work with frayed canvas edges.

Lightly sand all smooth, hard surfaces if you plan to glue a piece of needlepoint, fabric, or padding to it.

Spray adhesives are very good for adhering fabric to picture mats, cardboard liners for frames and books, etc., but they are really just a little too lightweight for gluing needlepoint work.

Tri-Tix Rubber Cream is my favorite. I'm usually impatient, and it is the quickest to use and easiest to clean from fingers and tools. You may have noticed I haven't mentioned several other popular adhesives. They have so many disadvantages that it's more worthwhile trying to get one of the recommended ones.

Sew

MACHINE STITCHING

Did you ever wonder why it seemed difficult to machine-stitch a straight edge on needlepoint, or why the needlepoint and fabric didn't match at the end of the stitching? Here's how to eliminate some of your problems.

It's difficult to sew close enough to the last row of needlepoint even with a zipper foot. When you sew seams by machine it's much easier if you work about two extra rows of needlepoint on all edges to be stitched. These are lost in the seam after stitching.

Use a zipper foot and keep the outer edge of the foot over and even with the outer row of needlepoint. Stitch slowly until you get the feel of it. If you try to stitch too close to the needlepoint edge, the foot usually drops off the needlepoint onto the unworked canvas and you have a crooked line of stitching.

One of the most important tricks to remember when machine stitching is to start sewing from the same end on both edges of a piece. Suppose you are making a belt. Start stitching at the pointed end of the belt, down the left edge to the buckle end. Cut your threads. Then start stitching on the right edge, at the pointed end.

The teeth of the feed dog pull the bottom layer from the front to back while the pressure foot is pushing the top layer in the opposite direction. The way professionals avoid this is to have a power machine with top and bottom feed. You can avoid it by proper directional stitching. Slick, flimsy, and diagonal-weave fabrics slide under the pressure foot more than fabrics without these qualities.

One other point to keep in mind is to clip corners only as you stitch to them. You can never predict exactly how fabric will feed through your machine. If you are stitching a bias welt to a straight edge, the problem is emphasized.

HAND SEWING

A curved needle and invisible thread are recommended. The thread's main advantage is also its greatest disadvantage. You can barely see it. Sewing with it is easier if you have one hand holding the needle and the other hand free to control the thread.

Start by turning seam allowances of unworked canvas underneath. Pin the two pieces to be joined to your blocking board. Seams should just meet, with the right sides on top. You are going to blind-stitch the two edges together from the right side. Run your curved needle under two threads of canvas (not wool) from the right-hand edge, then under two threads from the left-hand edge. Continue in this manner for the length of the seam.

To join linings to needlepoint, sew under two threads of needlepoint canvas and then take a small stitch in the fold of the lining. Alternate in this manner for the full length of the seam (see "Sleep Mask" chapter).

NEEDLE AND THREAD

Try to work with a thread long enough to complete the seam. Cut off twice the length of thread you need, plus one extra foot. If you use a single thread, it keeps slipping out of the needle and you can't anchor it well. Thread a curved needle. Knot the ends together with a figure-eight knot. Take your first small stitch in the seam allowance but don't pull it tight. Pass the needle between the two threads right below the knot and then pull it tight. Sew your seam. Fasten off by taking five or six tiny stitches right together and passing the needle under the last stitch before you pull it tight. That's all there is to it. You will be proficient after a practice inch or two.

If you are working with petit point and fine fabric, you can use a surgical needle. (See "Recommended Products.")

FIGURE EIGHT KNOT

1. Hold the ends of the thread in your right hand with the loop over the left index finger (Photo 7).
2. Turn your left hand toward yourself.

7

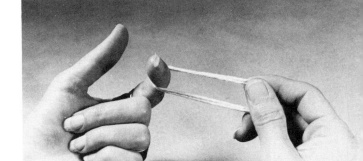

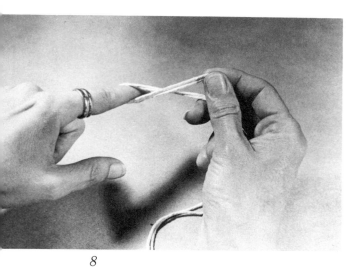

You will have one half-twist in the thread (Photo 8).

3. Continue turning your left finger toward yourself. You will have one full twist in the threads (Photo 9).

4. Pass the cut ends, from underneath, through the loop close to your left finger (Photo 10). Pull the cut ends tight and clip them to ⅛ inch.

8

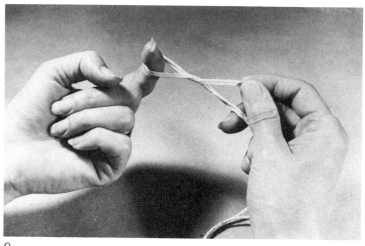

9

10

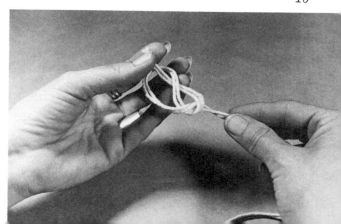

Care For It and Repair It

FABRIC PROTECTOR

I usually advise applying a fabric protector, such as Scotchgard, so cleaning will be reduced to a minimum. But fabric protectors are thin films which tend to hold stains if you rub them in. If the stain is merely a surface contact stain, it can be blotted off the needlepoint or fabric surface, provided you do this as soon as possible. Blotters or paper towels are good for this. Scotchgard will protect unglazed pictures, frames, and hangings from dust. All you have to do is vacuum them regularly. Be careful when you use a fabric protector. Spray several light coats just on the surface. Don't let it penetrate the yarns. I've seen it lift paints from the canvas right through the yarns, but I think it is worth this disadvantage.

CLEANING

Size, shape, and material will determine which method to use. Try to identify the stain. Is it water-soluble, or a grease spot?

Washable Articles

Follow the proportions of water to Woolite printed on the bottle. Do not soak; you will be asking for trouble. Lift the needlepoint in and out of the solution until it is clean.

Rinse the article in water of the same temperature it was washed in. Rinse several times, in clean water, until bubbles on top of the water pop immediately. If any cleaning solution remains, the bubbles on the surface of the water will take a few seconds to break. Any detergent left in the needlepoint will cause the colors to fade long before they should. Dust and gases from the atmosphere will be attracted to the fibers.

Roll the wet needlepoint in a dry towel. The towel should not have been washed in chlorine, as this will affect dyes. Hand-press as much moisture from the piece as you can. Block the damp needlepoint away from the sun or other source of heat.

COTTON:

Wash with Woolite in warm water. Rinse. Use peroxide for colored stains or mildew.

WOOL:

Wash in warm water not over 95 degrees. Rinse. Wool will shrink. Do not rub. Use no bleaches except peroxide.

SILK:

Wash in water temperature of 100 degrees with Woolite. Rinse. Do not use any bleach. Silk will shrink if not washed carefully. Dry cleaning is recommended.

METALLIC THREADS:

These are usually not washable. Synthetic metallic threads should be washed in the same way as wool.

SYNTHETICS:

Wash at 120 degrees in Woolite. Rinse. High temperatures cause yellowing. Synthetics have an affinity for attracting other colors and soil from water. Exposure to sun weakens colors as well as the fabric.

Bleaching. Hydrogen peroxide, 3 percent, is the only safe bleach for wool, silk, or cotton. It will remove mildew spots and some bleeding colors. Always use from a fresh bottle and do not put it in a metal container. Apply it with a medicine dropper to stained areas. Keep it moist and exposed to the sun until the stain is removed. You must rinse it well or it will continue to bleach. Always use the water temperature recommended for the fiber.

Nonwashable Articles

First, try to identify the stain.

Water-Soluble Stains. Try sponging the stain with a clean cloth dipped in cool water. When you must use a water and Woolite solution, use as little as possible. It is difficult to remove the excess without wetting a large area. Rinse thoroughly by sponging the spot with water or by forcing water through the stain with a syringe. You can also use alcohol instead of water to rinse the needlepoint. Test a small area to see if it is safe. It is easier to rinse out the detergent with rubbing alcohol, and the fabric will dry more quickly.

Grease Spots. There are no solvents available that will effectively remove grease spots without hazard to the user. Use them only in small amounts and in a well-ventilated area.

If it's possible, place the object, stained side down, on a pad of absorbent material. Press the back of the stain with a clean cloth pad dampened with grease solvent. Apply a small amount of solvent at a time. Work from the center of the stain toward the edges, to avoid rings. Keep moving the clean pad underneath, to absorb the grease and avoid transferring the stain back to the needlepoint.

Of course, if you can't work from the back of the object, all you can do is sponge it from the right side. Keep using a clean area of the dampened pad, so you don't transfer the stain back to the needlepoint.

GREASE SOLVENTS:
Perchloroethylene, trichloroethane, and trichloroethylene are nonflammable grease solvents. They are sold under various trade names. Exposure to vapors is dangerous to you.

NAPHTHAS:
Flammable. The names *petroleum distillate* and *petroleum hydrocarbon* may be used. They are available under various trade names; for example, Zippo Lighter Fluid. Avoid open flames, electrical equipment, and even static electricity.

GLAMORENE:
This is a grease solvent that contains both petroleum distillate and trichloroethylene. It is quite good for arti-

cles with permanent backings, such as chair upholstery, books, and frames. Sprinkle a layer over and beyond the spot. Rub lightly and press in with the back of a spoon, but don't rough the yarn. Allow to dry for a few hours and vacuum off.

TIP . . .

Do not use rug or upholstery cleaners with detergents. These all attract soil and you will have a spot bigger and better than the original stain.

REPAIRS: CUTS AND BURNS

MATERIALS:
Canvas threads removed from the edge of the needlepoint.
Matching yarns for damaged area

Note: Cuts are repaired in the same way as burns, except that you eliminate Step 1 below.

Step 1: Scrape away all charred canvas and threads (Photo 11).
Step 2: Unwork at least two rows of needlepoint stitches surrounding the damaged area. Cut the ends of these unworked stitches close.

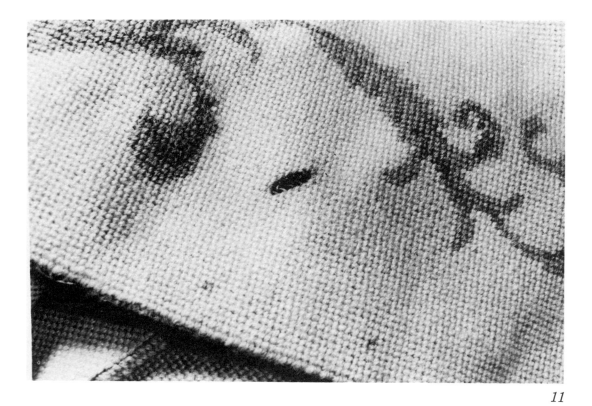

11

Step 3: Use a tapestry needle and re-weave the damaged canvas with a long, continuous thread. You have to duplicate the stitches that have been burned away or work over the ones that were cut. Start the reweaving from the wrong side, covering the two rows of undamaged canvas exposed where you unworked the needlepoint. You now have two canvas threads, side by side, in the undamaged area.

Step 4: Use matching yarn to duplicate the original needlepoint stitches. Begin to stitch over the top of the needlepoint stitches already worked. Begin at least two stitches beyond the rewoven canvas, over undamaged stitches remaining in the canvas. You will have to pull your wool tight over these previously worked stitches and the area of double-thread canvas repair. Do not pull your wool as tight

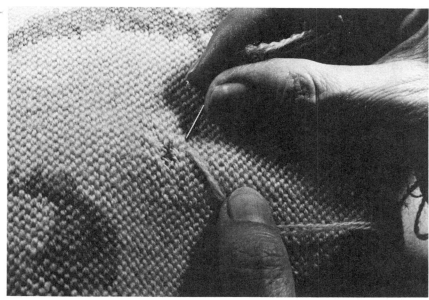

12

13

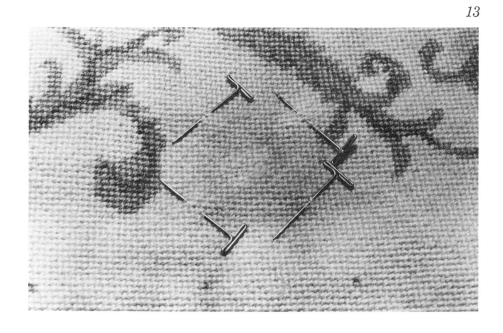

over the area of rewoven single-thread canvas (Photo 12). In some instances, if a two- or three-ply thread has been used for the original needlepoint, you may have to use one ply less for the repair.

Step 5: Mark off the repaired area with pins. Place the repaired section over a clean, folded washcloth. Moisten another clean cloth with dry-cleaning fluid. Press and blot the whole repaired area and a little bit beyond (Photo 13). This will help blend the repaired area with the old.

Step 6: Steam the area well and finger-press the area with the double-canvas threads.

SECTION II

FEMININE AND FUN

Briefcase

MATERIALS:

1⅓ yards canvas fabric, 36 inches
wide

⅔ yard interlining, heavy and stiff

4¾ yards ribbon, 1½ inches wide

½ yard lightweight belting,
1½ inches wide

Four heavy-duty Velcro fasteners,
⅞-inch size

One 14-inch zipper

Matching thread

Two pieces of thin cardboard,
6 inches by 4 inches

Step 1: Work a piece of needlepoint 16
inches wide by 24 inches long. Work
two pieces for handles 6 inches wide
by 4 inches high. Leave an unworked
area in the middle of each handle
3½ inches wide by 1¼ inches high.
This unworked area should begin 1½
inches from the bottom of the handle.

Step 2: Block all pieces of needlepoint
and trim unworked canvas to ½ inch
on the handles. Trim surplus canvas
on the large piece to within one row
of the needlepoint.

LINING

Step 3: Cut one piece of canvas fabric
21 inches long by 16 inches wide.

Step 4: Measure, press, and stitch a
¼-inch hem in each 16-inch side.

Step 5: Cut one piece of canvas 15½
inches long by 16 inches wide.

Step 6: Measure, press, and stitch a
¼-inch hem in each 16-inch side.

Step 7: Fold this piece in half, hemmed
sides together, and mark this fold line
as a guide (Photo 14).

Step 8: Fold and mark another guide
line across one half of this piece, from
the original guide line, to the hemmed
edge (Photo 14).

14

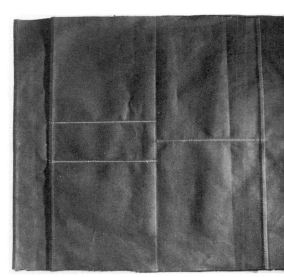

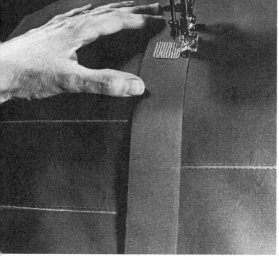

15

Step 9: Measure and mark two lines 7 inches from the raw edges, on each side, on the other half of this piece (Photo 14).

Step 10: Center this marked piece of canvas over the larger piece of canvas; cut edges matching and right sides facing up. Machine-stitch on your short marked lines to form pockets (Photo 14).

Step 11: Measure and cut another piece of canvas 16 inches wide by 25 inches long and a piece of stiff interlining the same size.

Step 12: Center and place this piece of canvas, with the interlining underneath, under the smaller finished piece with the pockets.

Step 13: Measure and cut a 16-inch length of ribbon. Position and sew one half of a Velcro fastener 3½ inches in from each end of the ribbon. Use the hook halves of the Velcro

here, so that when you remove the pouch from the case the hooks will not snag in things.

Step 14: Center this length of ribbon over the long marked guide line. Stitch along both edges of the ribbon through all layers (Photo 15).

Step 15: Position the halves of two more Velcro fasteners 1 inch down from the top edge and 3½ inches from both side edges. Stitch the fasteners in place through canvas and interlining. Sew the other halves of the fasteners in matching positions on the other short end of the lining.

HANDLES

Step 16: Cut two pieces of cardboard slightly smaller than the needlepoint handles. Clip the corners of the unworked canvas to eliminate bulk (Photo 16). Glue the canvas corners to the cardboard.

Step 17: Fold the outer unworked canvas over the edges of the cardboard

16

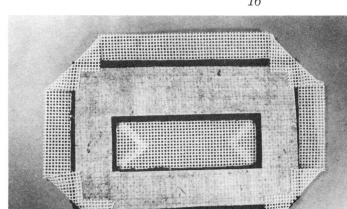

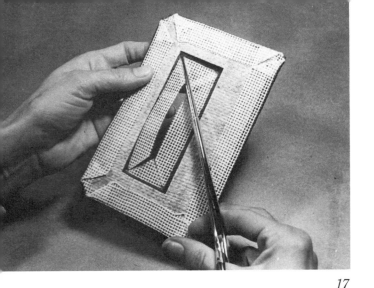

17

18

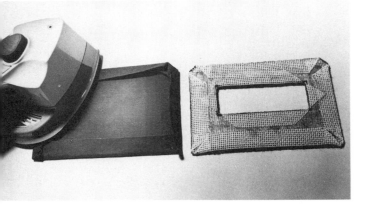

19

and glue in place. Put a line of glue on the unworked canvas, from each inside corner, toward the center. Allow the glue to dry (Photo 17).

Step 18: Cut the center area of unworked canvas down the middle and into the corners. Fold these edges back over the cardboard and glue them in place.

Step 19: Measure and cut a piece of canvas fabric 7 inches wide by 5 inches long.

Step 20: Place this piece of canvas over the handle and press the seam allowance under (Photo 18).

Step 21: Sew this piece of canvas to the back of the needlepoint around all outside edges.

Step 22: Mark and clip the unworked needlepoint canvas to the corners of the inside opening. Fold the seam allowance inside and stitch the edges of the opening.

JOINING

Step 23: Fold and steam-press a length of ribbon 82 inches long. Fold the ribbon down the center so one side is slightly wider than the other.

Step 24: Place the lining on top of the wrong side of the needlepoint. Put both of these pieces inside the folded ribbon binding and stitch in place. The narrower side of the ribbon should be on top. It doesn't matter if you stitch from the needlepoint side or the canvas side. Miter the corners of the ribbon as you come to them by folding a tuck on top and bottom. End the binding by folding the cut end of the ribbon inside ¼ inch and backstitch a few times (Photo 19).

Step 25: Center the handles at each end, on the needlework side. Line up the bottom of the handle opening with the top edge of the briefcase. Machine-stitch through all layers along the lower edge of the handle.

REMOVABLE POUCH

Step 26: Measure and cut a piece of canvas fabric 15 inches wide by 13 inches long. Fold this piece of canvas in half across the width. Measure and put a mark, on the long edge, 1¼ inches in from each end. Draw a line from this mark to the corner of the folded edge. Cut along this line (Photo 20).

Step 27: Measure and cut one 15-inch length of ribbon and one 15-inch length of belting.

Step 28: Open the piece of canvas. Center the belting and ribbon over the fold line. You can use double-sided transparent tape here to keep both pieces in position. Place the remaining halves of the Velcro fasteners on the ribbon to match the fasteners on the lining of the needlepoint. Sew the

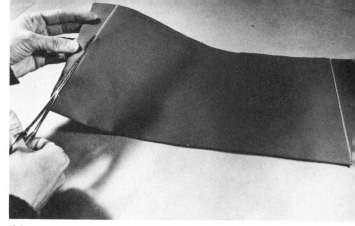

20

21

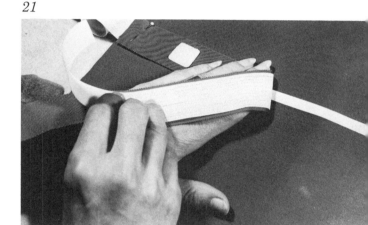

22

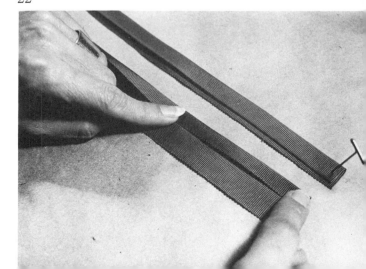

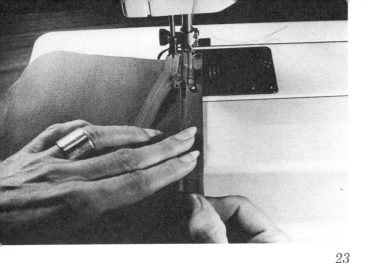

23

24

25

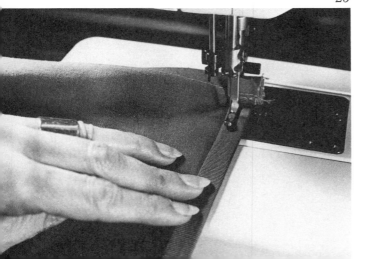

Velcro fasteners in place and stitch the ribbon and belting in place along the edges of the ribbon (Photo 21).

Step 29: Measure and cut two 13-inch lengths of ribbon. Fold and press the length of ribbon in half. Open the ribbon and fold one edge to the center fold line and press (Photo 22, bottom of picture). Fold the ribbon in half one more time (Photo 22, top of picture). Steam the folds in the ribbon.

Step 30: Place one half of the open zipper on top of the wrong side of the upper edge of the canvas, in the middle of the folded ribbon. Machine-stitch along the edge of the ribbon, binding the zipper to the canvas. Remember, the wider side of the ribbon should be underneath (Photo 23).

Step 31: Fold the other long side of canvas under, right side out, and attach the other half of the zipper with the binding (Photo 24).

Step 32: Measure and cut two 6-inch lengths of ribbon. Fold and steam-press as directed in Step 29 (Photo 22).

Step 33: Turn the folded pouch inside out and match the side raw edges. Cut zipper ends even with the canvas.

Step 34: Place the raw edges between the ribbon binding, just beyond the fold of the previously applied ribbon and belting. Machine-stitch the bind-

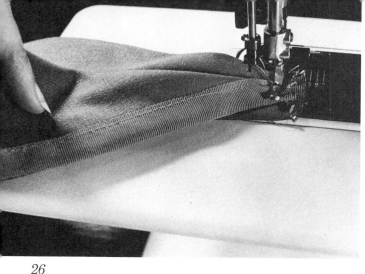

26

ing in place covering the bound ends of the zipper (Photo 25).

Step 35: Close the other end of the pouch as in Step 34.

Step 36: Flatten the unsewn end where the ribbon binding and belting meet. Stitch across everything to close the lower opening. Trim the seam (Photo 26). Close and trim the opening at the other end of the pouch. Turn the pouch right side out and press.

Step 37: The pouch is held in place in the center of the briefcase by the Velcro fasteners, and is removable (Photo 27). Spray the lining and needlepoint with fabric protector.

27

Evening Bag

MATERIALS:
    ¾ yard Pelomite or other nonwoven,
       iron-on interfacing
    Corded piping—purchase or make
       your own
    ½ yard lining fabric
    One skein of embroidery floss to
       match needlepoint

Note: All stitching is done with the zipper foot on your machine.

Step 1: Block needlepoint facedown.

Step 2: Cut out needlepoint, allowing ½-inch seams.

Step 3: Cut off all loose ends on back of needlepoint. They must be clipped close, so Pelomite will adhere properly.

Step 4: Iron Pelomite to back of needlepoint.

Step 5: Cut lining pieces using needlepoint as pattern.

Step 6: Cut one rectangular piece of lining fabric 4½ inches by 5½ inches for pocket.

Step 7: Iron Pelomite to back of lining pieces.

Step 8: Fold rectangular pocket piece in half with short ends meeting. Press. Position pocket piece on one side of lining. Stitch to lining around the three cut edges.

Step 9: Sew corded piping to right side around sides and bottom of both needlepoint pieces (Photo 28).

Step 10: Sew straight gusset piece to right sides of purse. As you sew the straight piece to the curved edge, you will have to clip into the seam allowance of the straight piece as you go (Photo 29).

Step 11: Sew lining the same way but take a wider seam allowance, as the lining has to be slightly smaller to fit inside the purse.

Step 12: Trim all but top seam allowances to ¼ inch on needlepoint and lining.

Step 13: Put lining inside purse, wrong sides together.

Step 14: Measure length of hinge side

28

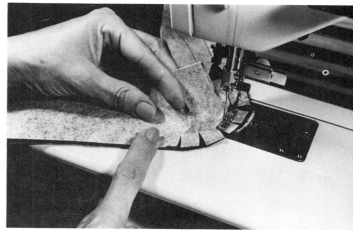

29

30

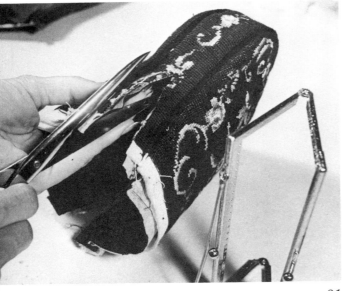

31

of frame plus ½ inch. Mark this measurement on gusset (Photo 30).

Step 15: Cut through needlepoint and lining gusset ends this measured distance.

Step 16: Trim this slash to within ⅜ inch from the seam on each side (Photo 31).

Step 17: Hold lining and needlepoint together and either zigzag-stitch or work the buttonhole stitch over the raw edges.

Step 18: Trim top seam allowance to fit frame.

Step 19: Fit bag into frame and hand-sew in place, using embroidery floss and the backstitch (Photo 32).

32

Lunch Box

MATERIALS:

   1-cup insulated jar (Thermos model
     #1155)
   Juvenile fork and spoon
   2 inches elastic
   14-inch zipper, open at one end
   ½ yard quilted lining fabric
   13 inches ribbon, ¾ inch wide

Curved needle and invisible thread
4¼-inch-by-4¼-inch piece of stiff
   cardboard
Zipper tape

Step 1: Work needlepoint to measurements shown (Pattern 1). Block and

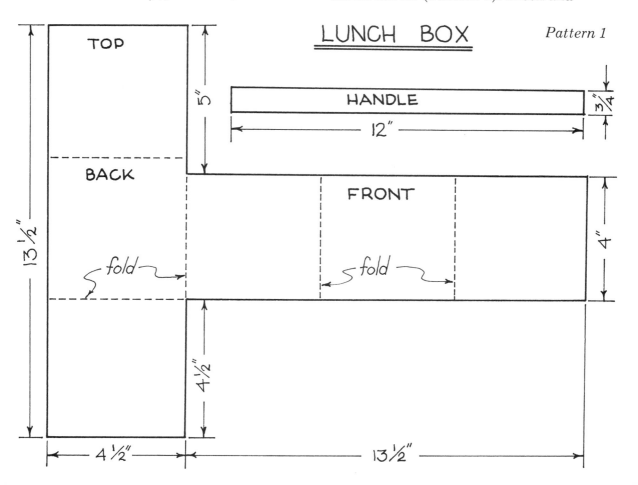

33

34

35

trim unworked surplus canvas to within ½ inch of needlepoint. Mark top, bottom, and sides on the surplus canvas.

Step 2: Cut a piece of stiff cardboard 4¼ inches square to fit in the bottom of the lunch box (Photo 33).

Step 3: Lay the needlepoint over the quilted lining fabric. Pin together and cut the lining the same size (Photo 34).

Step 4: Apply zipper tape to all edges of the needlepoint. Trim the corners and fold the surplus canvas over the tape and press in place. Be sure to have one row of needlepoint right on the edge of this fold (Photo 35).

Step 5: Begin blind-stitching the bottom to the lower edge in the corner (Photo 35). Continue to blind-stitch the bottom to the lower edge of the sides (Photo 36). Last, stitch on up the side, keeping the top edge even with the other side. Fasten thread (Photo 37).

Step 6: Fold the surplus canvas to the back on the long sides of the handle. Make sure one row of needlepoint is right on the edge. Press in place.

Step 7: Lay the handle over the ribbon and machine-stitch. Begin stitching at the same end on both edges of the handle.

Step 8: Place the ends of the finished

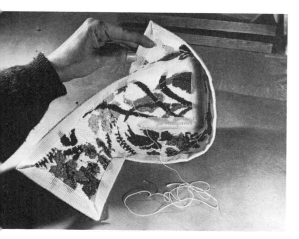

36

37

38

handle under the top about 2½ inches in from the front edge on both sides. Pin to secure in place and machine-stitch one row of needlepoint in.

Step 9: Open the zipper. Pin it under the edge of the top and machine-stitch it in place one needlepoint row from the edge. Stitch a pressure-foot distance from the corner, and make a small tuck in the zipper tape at the corner with the point of your scissors. Continue stitching to the next corner, make a tuck, and stitch to the end (Photo 38).

Step 10: Machine-stitch the other half of the zipper to the top edge of the lunch box. Catch-stitch both ends of the zipper tape securely by hand.

Step 11: Measure and mark the lining seams ¾ inch from the edge. Machine-stitch the lining seams on this line, clipping corners as you sew. Sew the last seam to within ¾ inch from the end. Try the lining inside the lunch box to make sure it fits. Trim the stitched seam allowance to ¼ inch.

Step 12: Make a clip at the unsewn corner (Photo 39).

Step 13: Fit the lining in the lunch box again. Use your spoon and fork as a guide to mark the position for the elastic on the right side of the top lining.

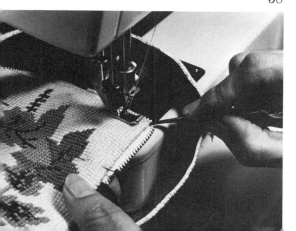

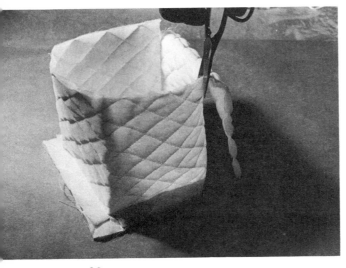

39

Step 14: Turn the ends of the elastic under and sew in place at each end and in the center.

Step 15: Insert the lining in the lunch box. Fold seam allowances inside and pin in place.

Step 16: Blind-stitch the lining over the loose edge of the zipper tape. Spray it with several light coats of a fabric protector. You have room for the thermos jar, a sandwich, and a napkin (Photo 40).

40

Needlework Case

MATERIALS:
  2 yards 36-inch canvas
  One matching 14-inch zipper
  Two Velcro heavy-duty fasteners
    (⅞ inch)
  ¾ yard ¾-inch ribbon
  ⅔ yard 2-inch ribbon
  Matching thread

Note: You can cut all pieces of canvas at one time, as in Steps 3, 6, 8, 18, and 24.

A one-way design would not be suitable, as the needlepoint is folded in half so you have two top edges.

Step 1: Work a piece of needlepoint 15 inches wide by 23 inches long. Notice the corners have been angled to eliminate bulk. If a pattern stitch is used, work one single row of needlepoint around all edges. Work two pieces of needlepoint 12 inches long by 1 inch wide. Block needlepoint.

ZIPPERED POCKET HALF

Step 2: Trim unworked surplus canvas to ¾ inch and press this edge to the wrong side. Have the last row of needlepoint right on the edge (Photo 41).

41

42

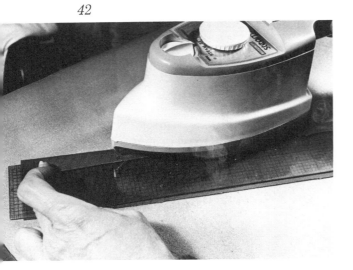

43

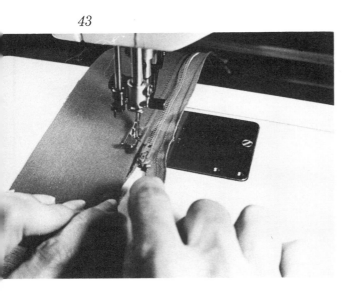

44

Step 3: Measure and cut a strip of canvas 16 inches wide by 2½ inches.

Step 4: Fold ½ inch of canvas, on the 16-inch side, over the edge of a ruler and steam this crease (Photo 42).

Step 5: Place one side of the zipper under this fold and machine-stitch in place. See that the zipper is centered lengthwise on this strip. Tuck the ends of the zipper tape under the folded edge as you stitch the beginning and end (Photo 43).

Step 6: Measure and cut a piece of canvas 16 inches wide by 11 inches.

Step 7: Follow Steps 4 and 5 to attach this piece of fabric to the other half of the zipper.

Step 8: Measure and cut another piece of canvas 16 inches wide by 7 inches.

Step 9: Fold and press one long edge, as in Step 4 (Photo 42).

Step 10: Fold this ½ inch under again and press (Photo 44).

Step 11: Machine-stitch this hem from the right side. You can put two rows of stitching along this hem if you want to.

Step 12: Find and mark the center of the long edge on this piece and the pieces with the zipper attached.

Step 13: Lay the smaller piece on top of the larger piece of canvas with the raw edges together.

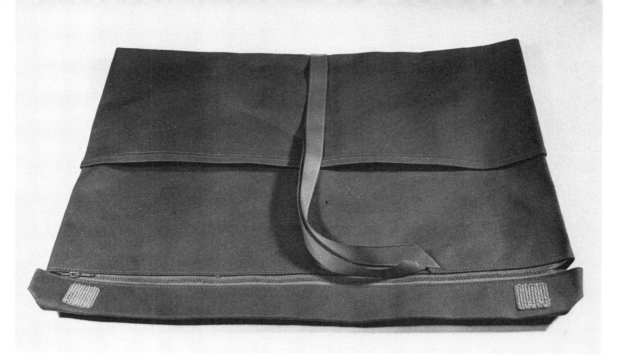

Step 14: Machine-stitch these together, down the center, from the hemmed edge of the top piece to the raw edges (Photo 45). This forms two pockets when completed.

Step 15: Lay this half over the needle-point and fold all raw edges under to match the edges and center of the needlepoint. Steam-press the seam allowances under.

Step 16: Fold the piece of ¾-inch ribbon in half and stitch the fold to the center bottom edge (Photo 45).

Step 17: Machine-stitch two halves of the Velcro fasteners to the narrow top strip above the zipper. Place them about 1½ inches in from the sides (Photo 45).

PLEATED POCKET HALF

Step 18: Measure and cut another piece of canvas 11 inches high by 22 inches wide.

Step 19: Follow Steps 9, 10, and 11 to hem one long edge of this piece.

Step 20: Make a 4-inch fold on the short edge toward the center, right sides together. Press this fold and machine-stitch its length on the *wrong* side.

Step 21: Make another fold, on the *right* side, 5 inches from the edge.

46

47

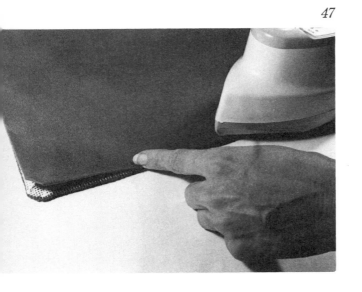

Machine-stitch its length on the right side (Photo 46). This forms a stitched pleat on one side.

Step 22: Repeat Steps 20 and 21 on the other short edge for a pleated pocket.

Step 23: Lay this piece over the needlepoint and press under the seam allowances as you did for the zippered pocket in Step 15.

Step 24: Measure and cut another piece of canvas 17 inches wide by 25 inches long for the interlining.

Step 25: Lay this piece of canvas over the needlepoint and steam-press under all seam allowances to match the needlepoint, as you did in Steps 15 and 23 (Photo 47).

Step 26: Fold this piece in half crosswise and lightly press the fold for a guide line.

Step 27: Lay the bottom edge of the zippered pocket half along this guide line. Machine-stitch this half to the interlining along this guide line and at all outer edges (Photo 48).

Step 28: Lay the bottom edge of the pleated pocket along this same guide line and machine-stitch the bottom and both side edges.

Step 29: Position the two remaining halves of the Velcro fasteners above the pleated pocket to match the other halves, and machine-stitch in place.

Completed inside of the needlework case will look like Photo 48.

HANDLES

Step 30: Cut away all unworked canvas right to the last row of needlepoint on the long sides of the handles. Fold ½ inch of unworked canvas under on the short ends.

Step 31: Center the needlepoint on top of a piece of wide ribbon. Fold the short ends of the ribbon under ¼ inch. Now fold one edge of the ribbon to the top, over the edge of needlepoint, and top-stitch close to the edge of the ribbon. Fold the other edge of the ribbon over to the top and stitch this side of the handle. Repeat for the other handle (Photo 49).

Step 32: Position the ends of the handles 5 inches in from both sides and 1 inch down from the top edge. Machine-stitch the ends in place on the right side of the needlepoint.

48

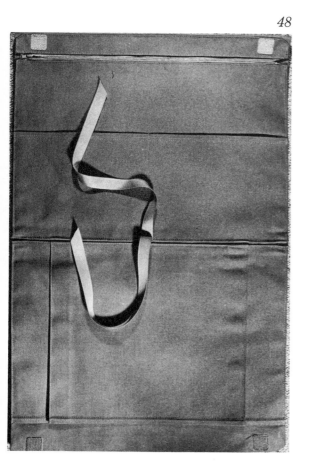

49

Step 33: Lay the completed lining over the needlepoint, wrong sides together, and blind-stitch the two pieces together on all edges (Photo 50).

Step 34: Spray the finished needlework case (Photo 51) with a fabric protector.

50

51

Overnight Bag

MATERIALS:

    ½ yard Ultrasuede for lining,
      36 inches wide

    ⅓ yard waterproof fabric for pockets

    1 yard Permette for interlining

    1 yard 1¼-inch ribbon

    One 18-inch separating heavyweight
      jacket zipper

    Two 7-inch zippers

    Four 1¼-inch "D" rings

    Two swivel snaps

    Four rivets

    Drive punch, setter, and
      small wooden block

    7-inch-by-9-inch piece of double-
      weight mat board

    Glue

    Masking tape

    Matching thread

Note: Ultrasuede is fairly expensive, so check steps 3, 7, 18, and 26. Arrange for the most economical layout. You don't have to worry about cutting with the nap.

Step 1: Work two pieces of needlepoint 14 inches high by 16 inches wide. Block needlepoint. Trim surplus unworked canvas to ½ inch.

Step 2: Blind-stitch the two side seams of the needlepoint pieces. Finger-press the seams flat. Fold and press the top edge of surplus canvas to the inside.

Step 3: Cut one piece of Ultrasuede, 8 inches by 10 inches, for the bottom of the bag. Round the corners. I used a quarter as a guide.

Step 4: Turn the needlepoint wrong side out. Machine-stitch the Ultrasuede bottom to the needlepoint sides, clipping the canvas corners as you stitch to them (Photo 52). Sew over the last row of needlepoint or the canvas will show.

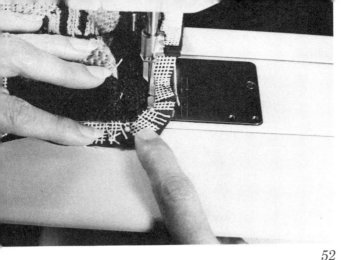

52

53

54

Step 5: Apply glue to the canvas and Ultrasuede seam allowance. Fold the seam over the needlepoint toward the top (Photo 53). Hold it in place with either spring clamps or clothespins until it is dry.

LINING

Step 6: Cut one long piece of Ultrasuede for the lining, 14 inches high by 31 inches wide. Cut another piece 7½ inches by 9½ inches.

POCKETS

Step 7: Five inches from each end, measure, mark, and cut two rectangular openings for the zippers, 7½ inches long by ½ inch wide. Cut these openings 8 inches from the bottom and parallel with the edge.

Step 8: Cut two pieces of waterproof fabric 15 inches long by 8½ inches wide for the two pocket linings.

Step 9: Apply zipper adhesive tape the full length of the bottom edge of one opening on the wrong side of the Ultrasuede. Center and finger-press one narrow end of the pocket lining to the zipper adhesive, wrong sides together. Apply another strip of zipper adhesive over this edge. Center the zipper, right side down, over the opening. Press the cloth edge of the zipper to the adhesive (Photo 54).

Step 10: Machine-stitch this lower half of the zipper in place on the right side of the lining.

Step 11: Apply zipper adhesive tape to the top edge of the opening. Press the other half of the zipper in place over this (Photo 55).

Step 12: Bring the bottom edge of the pocket lining over the zipper and finger-press this over the top edge of the zipper (Photo 56).

Step 13: Machine-stitch the ends and the top half of the zipper on the right side (Photo 57).

Step 14: Turn the Ultrasuede lining to the wrong side. Fold it out of the way and stitch over the ends of the zipper and down each side of the pocket to close it (Photo 58). The finished pocket, on the right side of the lining, will look like Photo 59.

Step 15: Repeat Steps 7 through 14 for the other pocket.

Step 16: Stitch the side seam of the lining ½ inch from the edge. Apply glue under the seam allowances and finger-press them flat.

Step 17: Measure and cut a piece of Ultrasuede 7½ inches by 9½ inches. Round the corners. Machine-stitch this piece to the bottom of the lining.

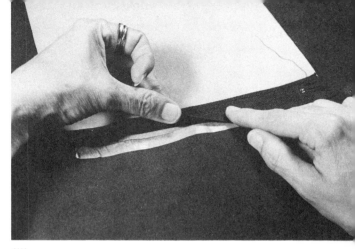

55

56

57

58

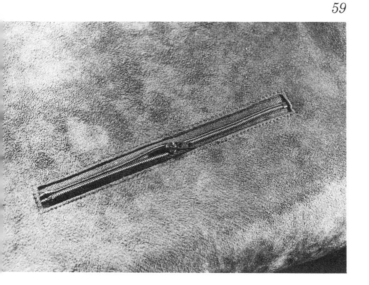

59

Trim the seam allowance to ¼ inch. The lining will look like Photo 60.

INTERLINING

Step 18: Cut a piece of Permette interlining 31 inches long by 8 inches high. Cut a piece of double-weight mat board 7 inches by 9 inches. Round the corners on the mat board.

Step 19: Overlap the short ends of the Permette ½ inch and secure with masking tape. Cover this seam with masking tape on the inside too. Cover the top edge of the join with masking tape also. Attach the mat board to the bottom edge with masking tape. Put another strip of masking tape

60

over this join on the inside for reinforcement (Photo 61).

Step 20: Drop the interlining into the
needlepoint covering. Put the lining
inside this.

Step 21: Work with one half of the
zipper at a time on each edge. Fit the
zipper on the top edge. Pin with a
few pins. Mark the zipper tape at a
point ¼ inch in from the needlepoint
seam. Clip half the width of the cloth
zipper tape at this point. This clip
will be about 2 inches from the separating end. Fold this last 2 inches of
cloth tape to the back and machine-
stitch along the folded edge.

Step 22: Apply zipper adhesive tape
to one inside canvas edge to hold the
zipper in place. Place the zipper half
fairly close to the edge over the adhesive tape. Apply another strip of
zipper adhesive over the cloth edge
of the zipper. Bring the top lining
edge beyond the zipper teeth and
finger-press it to the adhesive.

Step 23: Machine-stitch the zipper in
place from the right side between the
last two rows of needlepoint (Photo
62).

Step 24: Repeat Steps 21 through 23
to sew on the other half of the zipper.
Trim the lining to ⅛ inch from the
stitching line.

61

HANDLE

Note: The directions given here are for a convertible shoulder strap. You can change it to a short handle by slipping one "D" ring through the other and fastening the swivel hooks at one end. If you don't want a convertible strap, simply make the strap the length you desire and rivet it to the bag at each end of the zipper.

Step 25: Cut one length of Ultrasuede 1¼ inches wide by the width of the Ultrasuede. Cut another piece 1¼ inches wide by 32 inches long.

Step 26: Glue a length of ribbon to the back of the longest strip of Ultrasuede. Glue the shorter length of Ultrasuede to the ribbon beginning at one end. You will have a strap that looks like Photo 63.

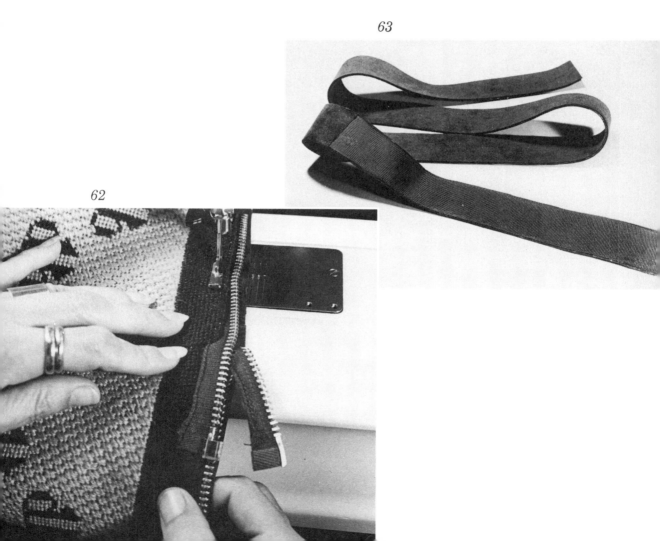

63

62

Step 27: Cut the strap at the end of the short piece of Ultrasuede. Put the eye of a swivel hook on a "D" ring.

Step 28: Fold 1 inch of the strap over the straight bar of the ring. Machine-stitch a 1-inch square to hold the ring in place. Repeat at the other end of the strap.

Step 29: Cut two 3-inch pieces from the remaining covered ribbon. Fold them over the bars of the last two rings and machine-stitch a 1-inch square on the ends of the ribbon (Photo 64).

Step 30: Put the small wooden block under the bag at one end of the zipper. Center the small tab over the seam with the ring just beyond the edge of the needlepoint. Use the drive punch to make a neat hole for the rivets. Set two rivets through all layers (Photo 65). Attach the re-

64

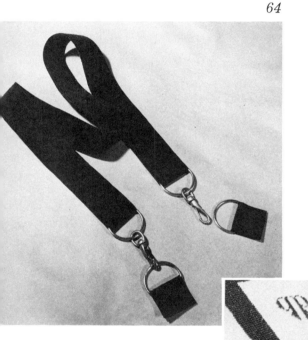

65

maining tab at the other end of the bag.

Step 31: Cut one piece of covered ribbon 2½ inches by 1¼ inches. Close the zipper and fold the ribbon in half. Glue the separating end of the zipper in the middle of this fold. Machine-stitch around the sides and bottom.

Step 32: For a final attractive touch, cut another 2-inch by ¼-inch piece of Ultrasuede. Put it through the hole in the zipper pull and glue the ends together.

Step 33: Steam the overnight bag and spray it with a fabric protector. The finished bag is shown in Photo 66.

66

Paperweight

MATERIALS:
 BBs for weight
 Glue
 Curved needle and invisible thread

Note: Top and bottom are worked in needlepoint.

Step 1: Apply glue to all edges of the blocked needlepoint right up to the stitches (Photo 67).

Step 2: Allow glue to dry and trim surplus canvas to within ¼ inch. Clip the canvas right to the needlepoint on all inside curves (Photo 68).

Step 3: Fold under all edges of the canvas on both bottom and top pieces of needlepoint and blind-stitch the two pieces together, leaving a small opening for stuffing (Photo 69).

Step 4: Fill the paperweight with BBs and close the opening (Photo 70).

67

52

68

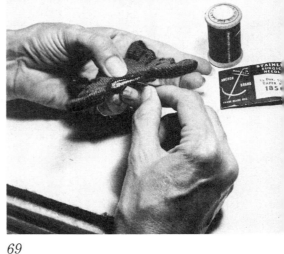

69

Note: A small item with a lot of inside curves, like the frog, is rather tedious to sew. Any design without curves, such as a ladybug, fruit, or mouse, would be more fun to mount.

70

Pet Bed

MATERIALS:

Fabric for back, bottom, bias welt,
and binding
½-inch-thick foam padding for back
and bottom
Cord for welt
Matching thread

Step 1: Make a paper pattern to fit
the inside back and bottom of your
pet basket. (See "Make a Pattern"
chapter.)

Step 2: Mark these outlines on canvas.
Work and block the needlepoint. Cut
away surplus unworked canvas to 1
inch.

Step 3: Use the needlepoint as a pattern to cut a piece of fabric for the
bottom.

Step 4: Cut a piece of fabric for the
back of the basket 2 inches longer
than the needlepoint at each end.
Use the needlepoint as your pattern.

Step 5: Cut a 2-inch-wide bias strip 2
inches longer than the opening at the
front of the basket.

Step 6: Fold this piece of fabric over a
piece of cord and machine-stitch the
length with a zipper foot to make a
piece of welt.

Step 7: Stitch the piece of welt to the
right side of the front of the bottom.

Step 8: Lay the piece of fabric for the
bottom over the needlepoint with
right sides together. Machine-stitch
only along the welt.

Step 9: Cut a piece of foam padding
for the bottom ¼ inch smaller on all
sides than the needlepoint area.

Step 10: Fold the attached piece of fabric under the needlepoint. Put the
padding between the fabric and the
needlepoint. Machine-stitch around
the padding, on the right side, from
one end of the welt to the other
(Photo 71). The bottom section will
look like Photo 72.

Step 11: Cut another 2-inch bias strip

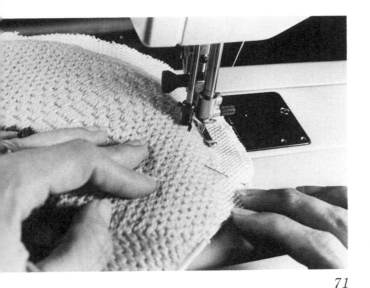

71

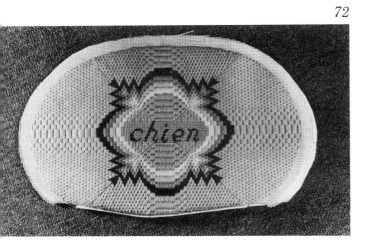

72

of fabric to fit around the top and sides of the needlepoint back.

Step 12: Fold this strip over a piece of cord and make a welt as you did in Step 6.

Step 13: Sew the welt to the top edge and ends of the needlepoint back (Photo 73).

Step 14: Machine-stitch the piece of needlepoint for the back to the bottom cushion. Clip the edge of unworked canvas as you sew (Photo 74).

Step 15: Cut a piece of foam padding to fit within the welt edge of the back. Pin in place here and there.

Step 16: Fold the top seam allowances under on the top edges. Begin pinning the fabric to the welt at the center top.

Step 17: Blind-stitch the edges together above the stitching line on the welt (Photo 75). Fold under the seam allowances on each end and blind-stitch these.

Step 18: Machine-stitch all layers together around the bottom edge from one end of the back to the other. Clip the edges of fabric as you sew to them.

Step 19: Cut another 2-inch-wide bias strip of fabric to fit around the bottom edge from one corner of the back to the other. Make a bias binding by

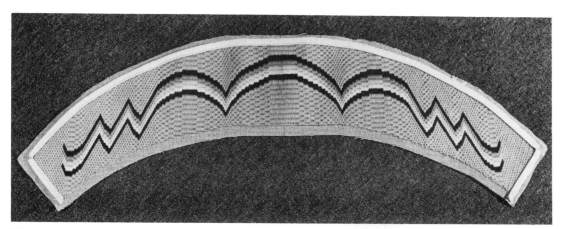

73

74

pressing a crease in the center length of the strip. Fold one raw edge to the center crease and press. Fold the other raw edge toward the center crease ¹⁄₁₆ inch less. One side of the binding should be slightly wider than the other. Press the completed binding.

Step 20: Trim the seam allowance on the bottom of the bed to ¼ inch.

Step 21: Fold in ¼ inch on one end of the binding. Insert the trimmed seam of the bed between the edges of the binding with the narrow side on top. Machine-stitch the binding in place beginning at one end of the bed back. Continue binding the raw seam edge all the way around to the other end of the back (Photo 76). Just as you sew to this last end, cut the bias binding ¼ inch longer than the seam. Turn this ¼-inch surplus inside before you sew to the end.

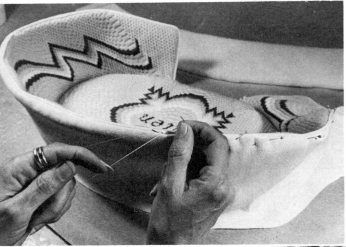

75

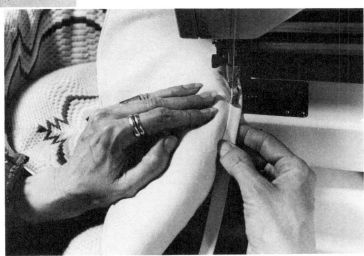

76

Step 22: Line the basket with waxed paper to prevent the steam from transferring varnish from the basket to the fabric. Steam the needlepoint, using blocking pins where needed (Photo 77).

Step 23: Allow the needlepoint to dry, and remove pins. Spray with a fabric protector. Pleasant dreams to the occupant (Photo 78).

77

78

Sleep Mask

MATERIALS:
- ¼ yard lining fabric
- 1 yard ribbon
- Matching or invisible thread
- Curved needle

Step 1: Block needlepoint facedown.

Step 2: Trim edges of surplus canvas to ½ inch wide.

Step 3: Fold these edges to the back of the needlework, steam, and pin in place (Photo 79).

79

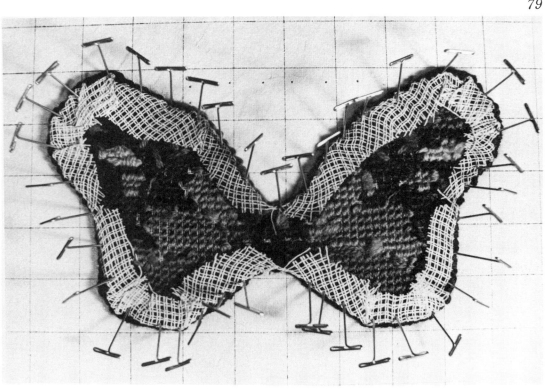

Step 4: Glue edges in place and apply pressure for neat edges (Photo 80).

Step 5: Use the needlepoint as the pattern for the lining. Cut the lining ½ inch larger than the needlepoint. Slash the edges of the lining to within ⅛ inch of the sewing line (Photo 81).

Step 6: Attach the ribbon to the back of both side edges of the mask either by machine or by hand (Photo 82).

Step 7: Put the mask, right side down, on a piece of blocking board or iron-

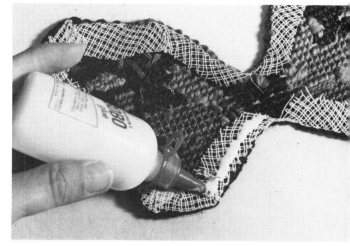

80

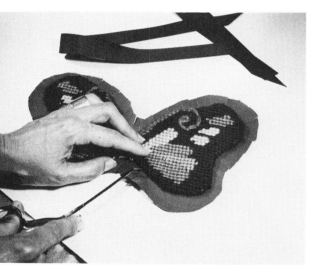

81

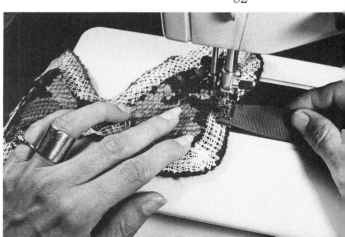

82

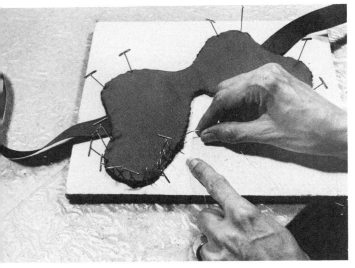

ing board. Position the lining and fold the raw edges to the inside. Pin in place on the board. Blind-stitch the lining to the edge of the needle-point canvas (Photo 83).

Step 8: Trim the loose ends of the ribbon on an angle to avoid raveling (Photo 84).

Suggestion: Line the sleep mask with plastic instead of fabric and use cotton pads moistened with witch hazel under the mask to refresh your eyes before a big evening.

83

84

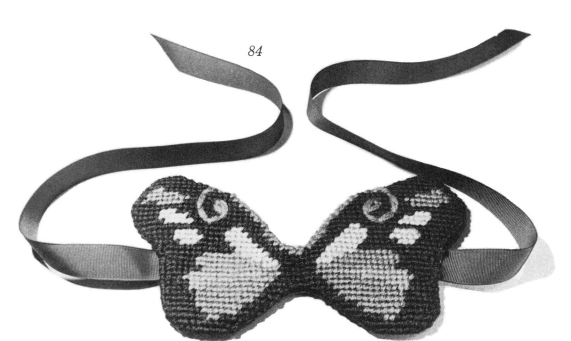

Take-Along

MATERIALS:

  ½ yard canvas fabric
  ⅔ yard ribbon, 1 inch wide
  7 yards ribbon, 1½ inches wide
  Two zippers, 14 inches long
  ½ yard upholsterer's clear plastic
  Matching thread
  Two Velcro fasteners

Note: If you prefer, you can cut all pieces of plastic, ribbon, and canvas at one time, as in Steps 4, 7, 9, 16, 18, 25, and 29.

Step 1: Work a piece of needlepoint 15½ inches by 24 inches.

Step 2: Block the needlepoint.

Step 3: Cut surplus unworked canvas to within one row of the needlepoint on all sides.

LINING

Step 4: Measure and cut one piece of plastic 15½ inches wide by 2 inches long. Cut one piece of wide ribbon 15½ inches.

Step 5: Fold the length of ribbon not quite in half (one side should be a tiny bit wider than the other) and steam-press.

Step 6: Place one long cut edge of the plastic in the middle of the fold and machine-stitch in place close to the edge of the ribbon. Have the wider edge of the ribbon underneath when it is sewn on.

Step 7: Measure and cut another piece of plastic 15½ inches by 9½ inches and one piece of wide ribbon 15½ inches long.

Step 8: Bind one long edge of the plastic, as in Steps 5 and 6.

Step 9: Cut another piece of plastic 15½ inches wide by 5½ inches. Cut two pieces of wide ribbon 15½ inches long and two pieces of narrow ribbon 5½ inches long.

Step 10: Measure and mark 5¼ inches from each short end toward the middle. Center the narrow pieces of ribbon across the plastic over these marks and machine-stitch the ribbon to the plastic. Stitch down each side of the ribbon.

Step 11: Bind one long edge of this piece of plastic, as in Steps 5 and 6. Cover the cut ends of the narrow ribbon with binding as you go.

Step 12: Lay this piece of plastic over the large piece, matching bottom and side unbound edges. Machine-stitch together through the center of the narrow pieces of ribbon. This forms three pockets when completed.

Step 13: Bind these two pieces together at the long cut edge with the remaining piece of ribbon, as in Steps 5 and 6 (bottom of Photo 85).

Step 14: Place one side of a zipper under the long bound edge of the narrow piece of plastic and machine-

stitch in place. See that the zipper is centered lengthwise on this strip. Tuck the ends of the zipper tape under the binding at the beginning and end.

Step 15: Place the other half of the zipper under the single bound edge of the large piece of plastic and stitch, as in Step 14. You now have the top half of the lining (Photo 85).

Step 16: Measure and cut a piece of plastic 15½ inches by 11½ inches. Cut one piece of wide ribbon 15½ inches long.

Step 17: Bind one long edge of this piece of plastic with the ribbon, as in Steps 5 and 6.

Step 18: Measure and cut another piece of plastic 15½ inches by 9½ inches.

85

Cut one piece of wide ribbon 15½ inches long and one piece of narrow ribbon 9½ inches long.

Step 19: Lay the narrow ribbon across the plastic in the center and machine-stitch in place on both edges of the ribbon.

Step 20: Bind one long edge of this piece of plastic with the wide piece of ribbon, as in Steps 5 and 6.

Step 21: Lay this piece of plastic over the larger piece, matching unbound edges.

Step 22: Machine-stitch the two pieces together in the center of the narrow ribbon (Photo 86). This is the bottom half of the lining.

Step 23: Place one half of the remaining zipper under the bottom bound edge (three pockets) of plastic. Machine-stitch the zipper in place, centering the zipper and tucking the tape ends under the binding at beginning and end. The top and bottom lining are joined with this zipper. All pockets must open from the top, so contents will not fall out when the take-along is hung up by its handle.

Step 24: Place the single bound edge of the other piece of plastic over the other half of the zipper and stitch in place.

HANDLES

Step 25: Cut four pieces of wide ribbon 14 inches long.

87

Step 26: Fold each piece in half length-wise and steam-press.

Step 27: Lay one piece of ribbon, with the fold on the left edge, inside another piece of ribbon with its fold on the right edge. Machine-stitch down both sides of the ribbon far enough in to catch loose edges. Make the other handle the same way. Fold the short ends of the handles under ¼ inch and machine-stitch.

Step 28: Place the ends of the handles 2 inches down from the top and 5 inches in from both sides on the outside of the needlepoint. Stitch a 1-inch square at the bottom of each handle.

INTERLINING

Step 29: Measure and cut a piece of canvas 15½ inches wide by 24 inches long.

Step 30: Lay the completed plastic lining over the canvas and machine-stitch together above the zipper and through the binding in the center of the lining, right at the bottom of the three pockets.

Step 31: Measure about 3 inches from each side and ¾ inch down from the top edge. Position the Velcro fasteners at these points and stitch in place. Repeat at the other end.

Step 32: Fold and press the remaining length of ribbon, as in Step 5.

Step 33: Lay the completed inside of the take-along over the needlepoint, wrong sides together. Trim the edges of plastic even with the needlepoint, if necessary.

Step 34: Bind the two pieces together by placing the edge between the folded ribbon and stitching through all layers. Miter corners when you come to them as you stitch by taking a tuck in the ribbon, top and bottom. You can stitch on either the lining side or the needlepoint side; just make sure you have the wider edge of the folded ribbon underneath and the handles folded out of the way (Photo 87).

Step 35: Spray the needlepoint with a coat of fabric protector and give it a light steaming if necessary. Remember, plastic is sensitive to heat.

Tennis Racquet Cover

MATERIALS:

One 12-inch zipper, open at one end
½ yard suitable fabric
3 yards purchased bias binding
1¼ yards corded piping

Note: All stitching is done with the zipper foot on your machine.

Step 1: Block needlepoint facedown.

Step 2: If needlepoint has been worked in a stitch other than basket weave, you will have to glue a piece of fabric to the back of the needlepoint to help it retain its shape. Trim edges right to needlepoint.

88

89

Step 3: Sew the corded piping to the right side of the needlepoint around curved edges. Do not sew piping across bottom straight edge (Photo 88).

Step 4: Pull out last ½ inch of cord from piping and cut this off (Photo 89).

Step 5: Cut one piece of fabric for the back. Use the front of the racquet cover for your pattern.

Step 6: Cut one strip of fabric 1 inch wide by 28 inches long.

Step 7: Sew the closed end of the zipper, right sides together, to the end of the 1-inch-wide strip. Turn fabric back and top-stitch this seam (Photo 90).

Step 8: Sew strip of fabric with zipper to right side of needlepoint over cording. Stitching should be on the same line as the piping.

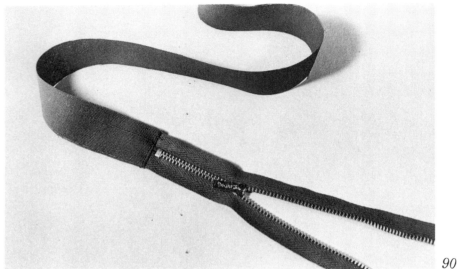

90

91

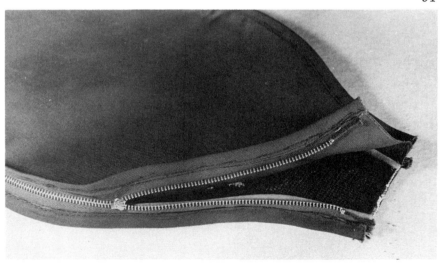

Step 9: Baste and stitch the bias binding over the raw edges of the needlepoint with the zipper strip already attached.

Step 10: Sew back piece of fabric to narrow strip.

Step 11: Baste and stitch bias binding over raw edges of this seam also. It is necessary to cover these seams so the straight piece of fabric does not ravel or get caught in the zipper (Photo 91).

Step 12: Turn tennis racquet cover right side out and sew bias binding over the remaining raw bottom edge (Photo 92).

92

Tote Bag

MATERIALS:
  Canvas fabric for lining
  Matching thread
  Stiff cardboard to fit bottom
    (optional)

Step 1: Block needlepoint. Trim unworked surplus canvas to ½ inch.
Miter corners and press unworked
canvas to the back, leaving the outside row of needlepoint right on the
edge (Photo 93).

Step 2: Cut one long piece of fabric for
the lining. The dimension for the
width will include the back, front,
and two sides plus ½-inch seam allowance at each end. The height of
this lining will include a ½-inch seam
allowance on the bottom, the height
of the needlepoint plus 1½ inches for
a top hem.
Step 3: Cut a rectangular piece of fabric for the bottom. The long sides will
be the width of your needlepoint plus

93

two ½-inch seam allowances. The short ends of the rectangle should measure the width of the side plus two ½-inch allowances.

Step 4: Fold and press a 1-inch hem on the top edge of the lining. Machine-stitch the hem.

Step 5: Cut one piece of fabric 5 by 7 inches for the inside pocket. Fold, press, and stitch a ½-inch hem in one long edge. Fold and press under a ½-inch seam allowance on the three remaining sides. Machine-stitch the pocket to the inside of the lining (Photo 94).

Step 6: Measure and mark guide lines on the outside of the lining for placement of the needlepoint pieces. Machine-stitch the needlepoint to the lining around all edges of needlepoint (Photo 95).

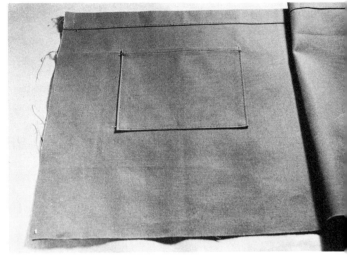

94

95

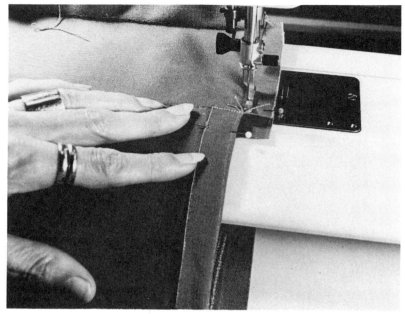

96

97

Step 7: Stitch the side seam allowance.

Step 8: Machine-stitch the fabric for the bottom to the sides, clipping corners as you sew to them (Photo 96). Trim the bottom seam.

Step 9: Cut two pieces of fabric 14 inches long by 3 inches wide for handles. Fold each piece in half lengthwise and press. Fold the ½-inch seam allowances inside and press. Machine-stitch both long edges of the handles.

Step 10: Measure and mark with pins the position for the handle ends on the top edges. Remove just enough machine stitches on the needlepoint to slip the handle ends between the lining and the needlepoint. Restitch on the same lines to secure the handles (Photo 97).

Step 11: Spray with a fabric protector. The finished bag is shown in Photo 98.

Step 12 (Optional): I like tote bags with a firm bottom; perhaps you do too. Cut a piece of stiff cardboard to fit inside the bottom of the bag. Cover it with some of the lining fabric, using spray adhesive. Lay this piece inside on the bottom. A loose inner bottom will not interfere with folding the bag flat.

98

Umbrella Cover

MATERIALS:
  ½ yard ¾-inch ribbon
  Nylon fabric for lining
  Glue
  Matching thread for machine
    stitching
  Invisible thread and curved needle
    for hand stitching

Note: Since umbrellas are tapered at one end, it is easier to make a paper pattern for your needlepoint outline. Steps 1 through 4 are directions for making the pattern for your particular umbrella.

Step 1: Measure around the top of the umbrella at the end of the ribs. Add 1 inch to this measurement. Mark this width on paper.

Step 2: Measure around the bottom of the folded umbrella and add 1 inch to this measurement. Mark this width on paper.

Step 3: Measure the length of the umbrella from the top of the ribs to the top of the bottom tip. Mark this length on paper.

Step 4: Take two more measurements around the umbrella at one-quarter of the length from both ends. Add 1 inch to these measurements and mark these on your paper pattern. You now have the dimensions for the area of needlepoint to be worked. You will notice your pattern is narrower at the bottom. If you work the needlepoint in a patterned stitch, be sure to work the last two rows on all edges in diagonal tent stitch.

Step 5: Work needlepoint to the above dimensions and block.

Step 6: Apply a line of glue ½ inch wide on back of needlepoint stitches and on at least two rows of unworked canvas on the top and bottom of cover. Allow to dry.

Step 7: Trim unworked canvas on seam

edges to within 1 inch of needlepoint.

Step 8: Fold these seam edges of unworked canvas to the back of the
needlepoint and steam in place.

Step 9: Trim the unworked canvas on
the top and bottom edges to the edge
of the needlepoint, leaving just one
row of unworked canvas (Photo 99).
These ends have been glued so they
will not ravel.

Step 10: Lay the needlepoint over the
lining fabric. Cut the lining 1 inch

wider than the seam edges of the
needlepoint and even with the top
and bottom edges.

Step 11: Machine-stitch a length of ribbon to the bottom edge of the cover,
from the right side, through the needlepoint and lining. Have your ribbon
extend at least 1 inch beyond each
end of stitching. Position it on the
edge so it covers two or three rows of
needlepoint. The ribbon will be folded
over and stitched from the back

99

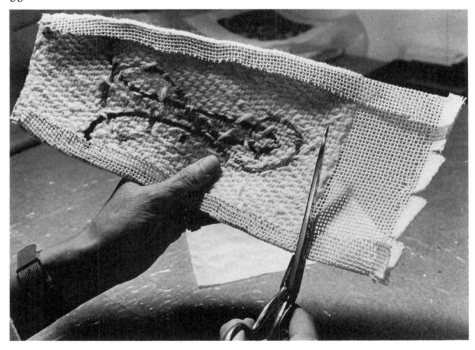

again, so it must be wide enough for this (Photo 100).

Step 12: Turn needlepoint over. Fold ribbon over raw edges from the front and machine-stitch, on the lining side, through all layers (Photo 101).

Step 13: Repeat Steps 11 and 12 on the top end of the cover.

Step 14: Fold the cover in half lengthwise with the lining sides together, but have the lining extend beyond the needlepoint edge. Stitch the full

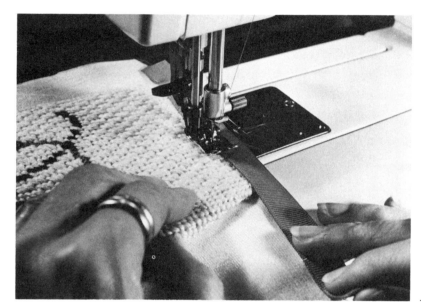

100

101

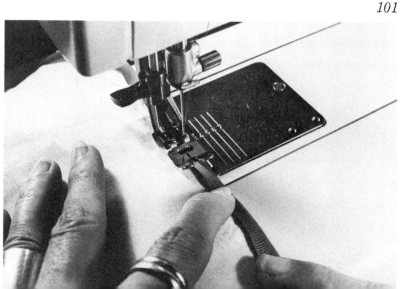

length of the lining (Photo 102).

Step 15: Open the seam of the lining and press to each side of the seam (Photo 103).

Step 16: Tuck the surplus ends of the ribbon between the lining and the needlepoint. Use invisible thread and a curved needle and anchor your thread through the ribbon.

Step 17: Fasten the ribbon together with a few stitches and continue to blind-stitch the entire seam from the

102

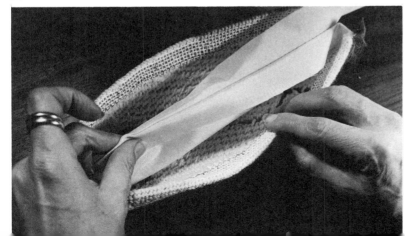

103

right side of the needlepoint (Photo 104). Tuck the remaining surplus ends of the ribbon inside and anchor the thread through the ribbon and needlepoint.

Step 18: Lightly steam the seam flat and spray with a fabric protector. Slide cover over umbrella (Photo 105).

104

105

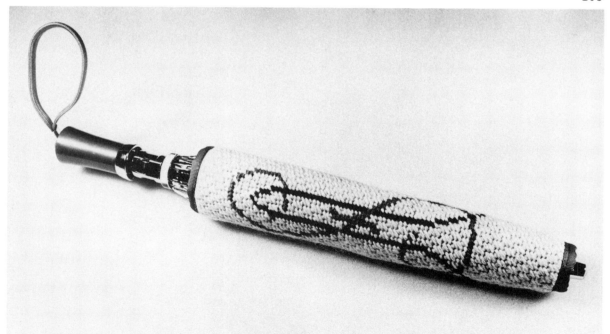

FOR MEN

Bookends

MATERIALS:

    Purchased bookends

    Lining fabric (I have used a synthetic suede cloth that will not ravel. It can be cleanly trimmed and edges do not have to be turned under.)

    Glue

    Pressure boards

    Four "C" clamps

Note: The bookends used here were already padded and covered with plastic-coated paper. If you don't buy padded bookends, simply glue a ¼-inch-thick piece of polyfoam padding to the entire face of the bookends and proceed from there, omitting Step 2.

Step 1: Measure the top and bottom edges and the height of the bookends. Measure the side edges and the width. These measurements, plus one additional row on all edges, are the outline for the finished needlepoint. Work the needlepoint to these measurements and block.

Step 2: Sand the face and sides of the bookends to get a rough surface so the glue will form a close bond (Photo 106).

Step 3: Apply glue to four rows of unworked canvas at the lower needlepoint edge and allow it to dry. Put the glue right up to the needlepoint (Photo 107). This prevents raveling.

Step 4: Cut out two rows of unworked canvas, which has been glued, at each lower corner (Photo 108).

Step 5: Position the needlepoint on the front of the bookend and glue it in place. Apply pressure for a tight bond.

Step 6: Fold the side edge of unworked canvas to the back of the bookend (Photo 109). Trim the top corners of the canvas to eliminate bulk. Apply

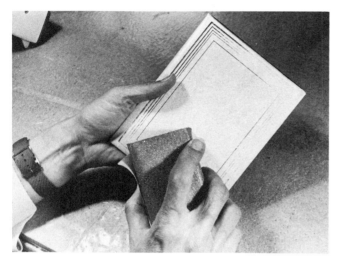

106

107

108

109

110

111

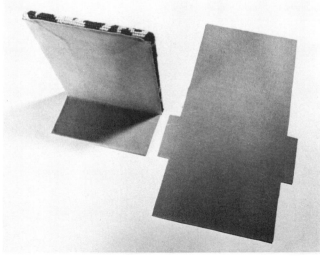

glue and pressure. Repeat for the other edge of the bookend.

Step 7: Follow Step 6 for each remaining edge. The back of the bookend will look like Photo 110.

Step 8: Trim the lower edge of unworked canvas even with the bottom front edge of the bookend and glue it in place.

Step 9: Cut the lining fabric slightly larger than the back and bottom of the inside of the bookend. Cut the projections that wrap over the sides of the bottom ½ inch wide (right side of Photo 111).

Step 10: Glue the lining to the top of the bottom. Fold the two projections to the bottom and glue in place (Photo 112). Apply pressure. Glue the bottom and back next (left of Photo 111).

Step 11: Trim the edges of the lining even with the needlepoint, and spray the finished bookends (Photo 113) with a fabric protector.

112

113

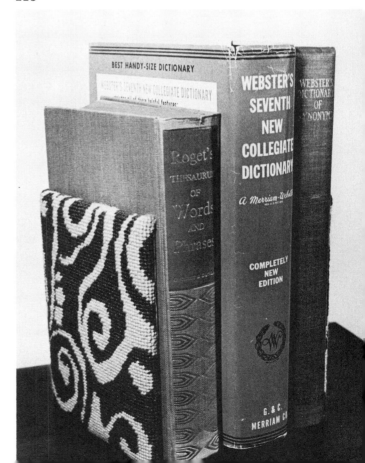

Bottle Carrier

MATERIALS:
- ½ yard quilted lining
- 1½ yards 1½-inch ribbon
- One 14-inch zipper
- String for ribbon piping
- Zipper adhesive tape
- Matching thread

Step 1: Work needlepoint to measurements in pattern (Pattern 2). Block needlepoint. Trim the unworked surplus canvas to ½ inch.

Step 2: Apply glue to the center strip of unworked canvas in the front piece of needlepoint. Allow to dry.

Step 3: Cut the strip of unworked canvas down the center and diagonally into each corner (Photo 114). Fold the edges of the unworked strip to the back and steam-press.

Step 4: Apply zipper adhesive tape all around the back of this opening. Center the zipper and finger-press it in place over the adhesive. Machine-stitch the zipper from the right side (Photo 115).

Step 5: Apply glue right up to the needlepoint on both long edges of the handle. Allow to dry, and trim surplus unworked canvas to within one thread of the needlepoint.

Step 6: Cut a piece of ribbon the same length as the handle. Machine-stitch one edge of the ribbon over one edge of the needlepoint handle. Fold the ribbon under the handle and stitch the other edge (Photo 116). Don't forget to start stitching both edges from the same end.

Step 7: Stitch each end of the handle to the front top of the carrier, even with the top of the zipper (Photo 117).

Step 8: Fold the remaining piece of ribbon in half lengthwise over the string and machine-stitch the length to make the piping.

BOTTLE CARRIER

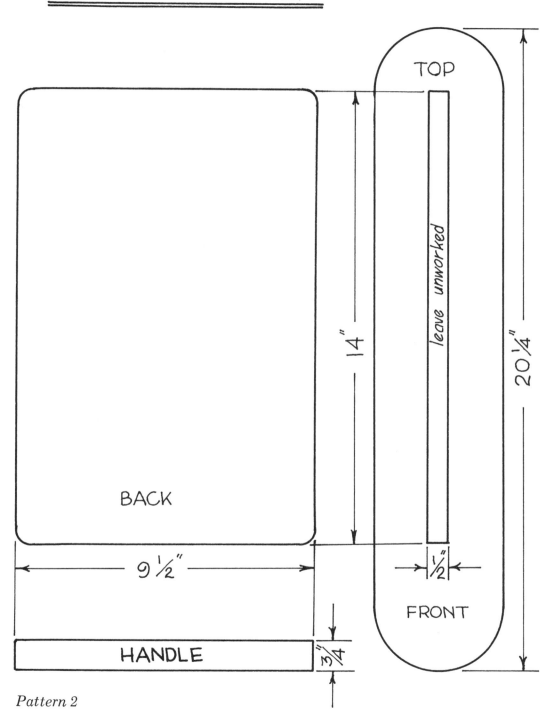

TOP

leave unworked

14"

20¼"

BACK

9 ½"

½"

FRONT

HANDLE

¾"

Pattern 2

114

Step 9: Stitch the piping around the
  edge of the rectangular back piece of
  needlepoint.
Step 10: Pin both pieces together and
  blind-stitch to the piping (Photo
  118).
Step 11: Use both pieces of needlepoint

115

116

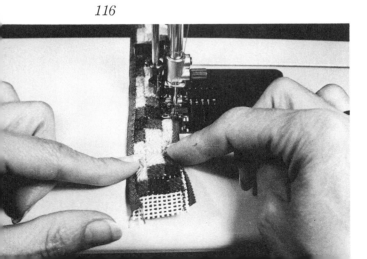

as patterns for the lining. Cut the lining. Mark and cut the zipper opening in the lining.

Step 12: Machine-stitch the lining together. Trim the stitched seam allowance to ¼ inch (Photo 119).

Step 13: Place the lining in the carrier.

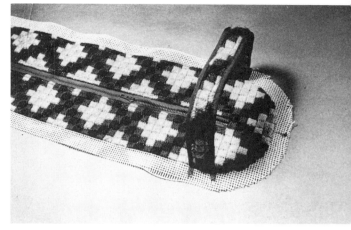

117

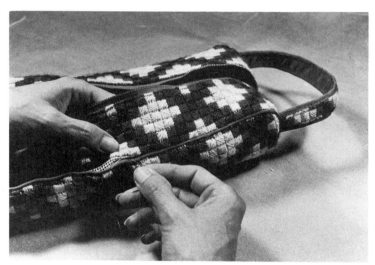

118

119

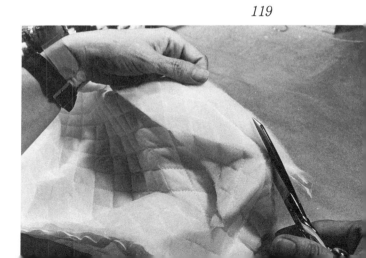

Turn under the seam allowance of
the zipper opening and pin in place
over the edges of the zipper tape
(Photo 120).

Step 14: Blind-stitch the lining to the
zipper tape.

Step 15: Spray the finished carrier
(Photo 121) with a fabric protector.

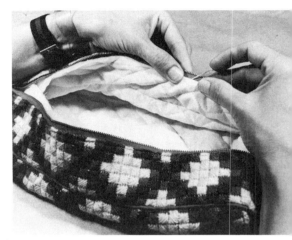

120

121

Cummerbund

MATERIALS:

    ¼ yard satin fabric
    ¼ yard medium-weight woven
      interfacing
    ½ yard nonroll elastic, 1 inch wide
    One 1-inch bra fastener

Step 1: Make a paper pattern to determine the needlepoint area to be worked. The cummerbund measures 15¼ inches long by 4¾ inches high, tapering to 3¾ inches at each end. Start the curved taper line 5 inches in from each end on the bottom line and 4 inches in from each end on the top line. Mark the outline on paper.

Step 2: Transfer this outline to the needlepoint canvas and work within this area. Block needlepoint.

Step 3: Trim surplus unworked canvas to within ½ inch of needlepoint.

Step 4: Make a pattern for the satin ends of the cummerbund. Measure and mark, on paper, an area 5½ inches long by 4¾ inches high at one end, tapering to 2 inches at the other end. Cut this pattern out.

Step 5: Use this pattern to cut a pair of satin ends. Use this same pattern to cut a pair of interlining ends. Cut the elastic in half.

Step 6: Lay the satin, with the right side on top, over the interlining. Center one cut end of the elastic over the satin on the narrow end. Machine-stitch through elastic, satin, and interlining (left side of Photo 122).

Step 7: Place this unit over the end of the needlepoint, right sides together, and machine-stitch through all layers

122

over one row of needlepoint (right side of Photo 122).

Step 8: Repeat Steps 6 and 7 for the other end of the cummerbund. Press the satin ends out flat.

Step 9: You don't have to make a paper pattern for the back. Simply lay the needlepoint, with attached ends, on the remaining piece of satin and cut around all edges.

Step 10: Lay this piece of satin over the needlepoint with right sides together. Machine-stitch around all edges, over one row of needlepoint. Leave about a 4-inch opening in the center of the bottom edge.

Step 11: Turn the cummerbund right side out. Blind-stitch the bottom opening closed.

Step 12: Thread one cut end of elastic through the bra fastener. Fold the elastic to suit the individual measurements of the wearer. Machine-stitch the bra fastener in place near the fold. Fold the cut end of the other piece of elastic under about 1 inch. Turn the raw end under and machine-stitch about ½ inch from the fold to make the loop for the fastener (Photo 123).

Step 13: Steam-press the completed cummerbund, and spray lightly with a fabric protector (Photo 124).

123

124

Desk Blotter—Covered Ends

MATERIALS:
  Purchased blotter
  Spray adhesive
  Glue
  Brown wrapping paper

Step 1: Measure the top and overall sides of area to be covered. Work needlepoint to this size and block. Trim surplus unworked canvas to at least 1 inch from edges of needlepoint.

Step 2: Apply a line of glue to the corners of unworked canvas on one edge of the needlepoint (Photo 125).

125

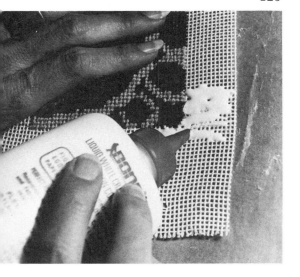

Spread the glue right up to the last row of needlepoint. This is where the canvas will be cut and slipped under the edge of the blotter ends. Allow the glue to dry.

Step 3: Position the needlepoint along the inside edge of the end to be covered. Clip out a row or two of unworked canvas, at each end, right to the points that will allow you to slide the unworked canvas under the edge of the blotter end (Photo 126).

Step 4: Slide a piece of waxed paper between the unworked canvas and the base. Apply glue and pressure. Allow the glue to dry.

126

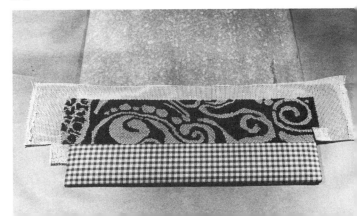

Step 5: Fold the two ends of unworked canvas to the center and glue in place (right side of Photo 126).

Step 6: Fold the three sides of unworked canvas to the bottom of the blotter and glue them in place. Apply

pressure and allow to dry (Photo 127).

Step 7: Repeat Steps 3 through 6 for the other end of the blotter.

Step 8: Cut a piece of brown wrapping paper the size of the bottom of the blotter. The paper should cover all unworked canvas edges. Spray the bottom of the blotter with adhesive and carefully lay the brown paper in place, beginning at one end. Apply pressure with a rolling pin over the paper for a tight bond.

Step 9: Spray the needlepoint ends with a light coat of fabric protector and insert a blotter (Photo 128).

127

128

Hatband

MATERIALS:
  ¾ yard ribbon
  Matching or invisible thread

Step 1: Sew the ends of the blocked band together with either a decorative stitch (binding stitch was used here) or blind stitch. Trim surplus canvas to ½ inch.

Step 2: Open the seam and steam it flat (Photo 129).

Step 3: Fold the edges of surplus canvas to the back and steam.

129

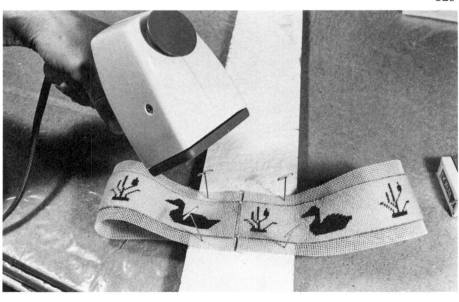

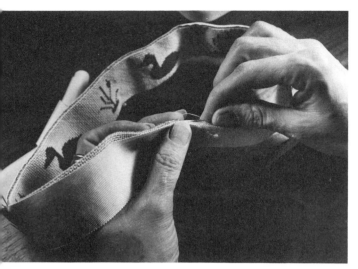

Step 4: Blind-stitch the ribbon to the needlepoint edges (Photo 130).

Step 5: Place the hatband on the hat and tack it in place from inside the hat at center front and center back (Photo 131).

130

131

Letter Holder

MATERIALS:
  Purchased letter holder
  Fabric for lining
  ¼-inch-thick polyurethane foam
    padding
  Glue

Step 1: Sand the outer surfaces of the letter holder. The surface needs to be slightly rough for the glue to hold.

Step 2: Cut pieces of foam padding to fit the front and back of the holder.

Step 3: Spread glue over one side of the holder and position the padding in place (Photo 132).

Step 4: Spread a small amount of glue on the unworked needlepoint canvas at each side of the bottom two rows of needlework where it will be cut later on, in Step 7. Allow to dry (Photo 133).

Step 5: Position needlepoint on the front of the holder. Glue the unworked canvas to the top inside edge of the holder.

132

133

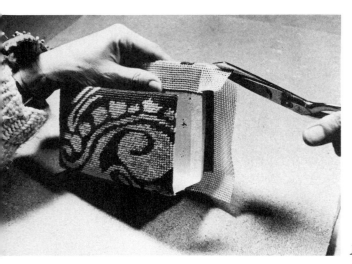

134

135

136

Step 6: Clip out the corners of un-worked canvas at the top sides (Photo 134). Glue the side edges in place.

Step 7: Clip out two rows of unworked canvas at both bottom edges, right next to the last two rows of needle-point. This is where the needlepoint folds to the bottom. Glue this bottom edge last.

Step 8: Repeat Steps 3 through 7 for the other half of the letter holder.

Step 9: Measure the inside of the letter holder for your lining pattern. Allow for two ½-inch flaps to cover the edges of the bottom (Photo 135). I find it easier to cut this lining slightly larger than needed, about ¼ inch, and trim it to the exact size after it is glued.

Step 10: First, glue the lining to the in-side bottom of the holder.

Step 11: Fold the flaps to the outside bottom and glue in place.

Step 12: Next, glue the sides of the lin-ing in place.

Step 13: Cut a piece of lining to fit the outside bottom of the holder and glue this in place last (Photo 136).

Step 14: Trim all edges of lining evenly (Photo 137).

137

Pencil Cup

MATERIALS:
  Purchased pencil cup
  ¾-inch-wide ribbon to fit around top
    and bottom of cup
  Glue
  Clothespins, rubber bands, and
    lightweight cardboard

Step 1: Lightly sand the outside of the
  pencil cup.

Step 2: Trim surplus unworked canvas
  to ¼ inch on all edges of needlepoint.

Step 3: Fold the long edges to the back.
  Steam and glue them in place, so one
  row of needlepoint is right on the
  edge.

Step 4: Clip out unworked canvas at
  corners (bottom of Photo 138).

Step 5: Cut ribbon in half lengthwise.

Step 6: Fold one piece of ribbon under
  ¼ inch at one end. Glue this piece of
  ribbon over the top rim of the cup
  with the turned-under end covering
  the other cut end of the ribbon. Hold

ribbon in place with clothespin until
the glue is dry (top of Photo 138).

Step 7: Fold the remaining piece of ribbon in half lengthwise and turn under
  ¼ inch at one end. Press.

138

139

Step 12: Wrap the cardboard around the cup and hold it in place with rubber bands. Apply pressure to the top rim with clothespins (Photo 139). Allow to dry.

Step 13: Remove clothespins, rubber bands, and cardboard. Spray the finished cup (Photo 140) lightly with a fabric protector.

140

Step 8: Glue this piece of folded ribbon to the lower edge of the cup with the fold of the ribbon on the bottom and the turned-under end covering the cut end. Hold in place with a wide rubber band until the glue is dry.

Step 9: Fold the unworked canvas under on both short ends of the needlepoint.

Step 10: Glue the needlepoint around the cup, covering the edges of the ribbon on the rims.

Step 11: Cut a piece of lightweight cardboard (I used an old file folder) to fit around the cup.

Tobacco Pouches

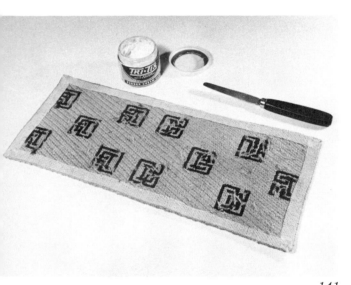

141

142

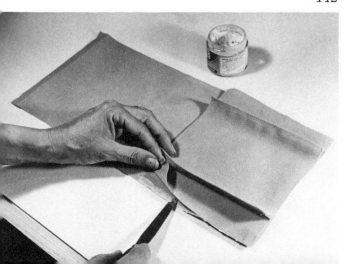

METHOD I

MATERIALS:
    ¼ yard plastic-coated cloth or plastic
    Matching thread
    Pressure boards
    "C" clamps
    Waxed paper
    Glue

Step 1: Work needlepoint to desired size plus one additional row on all sides. Block.

Step 2: Trim unworked canvas to within ½ inch of needlepoint.

Step 3: Lay needlepoint over lining fabric and cut lining fabric to this size. Lay aside.

Step 4: Turn the unworked canvas and the extra one row of needlepoint to the back. Steam in place.

Step 5: Miter corners and glue these edges in place (Photo 141). Apply pressure and allow the glue to dry.

Step 6: Cut another piece of lining fabric one-third the length of the first piece and 2 inches wider.

Step 7: Fold ¼ inch under on one long side (top) of this piece and machine-stitch close to the edge.

Step 8: Form a stitched pleat by folding about 3 inches under on the left half of this piece. Machine-stitch the full length of this fold, close to the fold.

Step 9: Make another fold an inch from the first stitched fold, away from the center. Machine-stitch this fold close to the edge on the inside.

Step 10: Repeat Steps 8 and 9 on the right half of this piece.

Step 11: Spread a little bit of glue under the raw edges to hold this pocket to the lining (Photo 142).

Step 12: Turn under all edges of the lining and pocket to fit the needlepoint.

Step 13: Machine-stitch the lining to the needlepoint close to the edge (bottom left of Photo 143).

METHOD II

MATERIALS:
  Purchased plastic pouch
  Thread to match needlepoint

Step 1: Work needlepoint one row larger on all sides than purchased tobacco pouch and block the finished needlepoint.

Step 2: Trim unworked canvas to within ½ inch of needlepoint.

Step 3: Turn unworked canvas and one row of needlepoint to the back. Steam in place.

Step 4: Miter corners and glue these edges in place (Photo 141). Apply pressure.

143

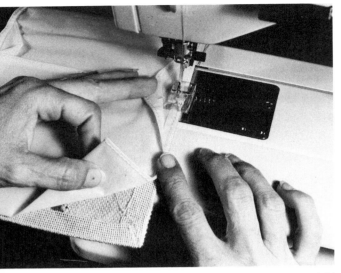

144

Step 5: Lay purchased pouch over wrong side of needlepoint and machine-stitch next to the edge (top right of Photo 143). You will have to lift the needle and pressure foot for one stitch length when you reach the bottom of the gusset in the side of the pouch (Photo 144).

Both pouches: Fold pouch in thirds and lightly steam the folds (Photo 145). I put a heavy weight on the pouches overnight, after they were steamed. You can also put the pouch between the pressure boards until the folds are set. Spray lightly with a fabric protector.

145

AROUND THE HOUSE

Bench Pad

146

147

MATERIALS:
   Fabric for back of cushion and welt
   Cord for welt
   Padding
   1-inch-wide elastic
   Two 1-inch bra fasteners
   Matching thread

Step 1: Block needlepoint and trim unworked surplus canvas to ½ inch.

Step 2: Cut enough 2-inch-wide bias strips of fabric to fit around the cushion. Seam the strips together at the ends. Fold the fabric strip over the cord and machine-stitch close to the cord with the zipper foot.

Step 3: Begin machine stitching the welt, 1 inch from the end of it, to the right side of the cushion at the center of the bottom. Clip the welt as you sew to the corners (Photo 146).

Step 4: End your stitching of the welt

by lapping the end over the beginning at an angle (Photo 147).

Step 5: Cut the elastic into four equal pieces. If the bench has a hinged top, measure the distance between the hinges. Place two pieces of elastic to one edge so they will be between the hinges. Machine-stitch the ends of the elastic in place over the cording in the same line of stitching (Photo 148).

Step 6: Repeat Step 5 on the opposite edge of the cushion, using the remaining two pieces of elastic.

Step 7: Cut a piece of fabric for the back the same size as the needlepoint and its seam allowances.

Step 8: Machine-stitch this piece of fabric to the needlepoint, right sides together. Make sure your elastic ends are tucked inside. Stitch with the fabric on top in the same line of stitch-

148

149

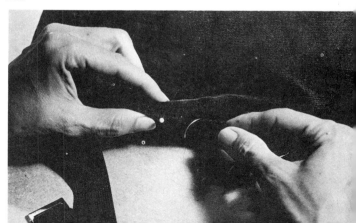

ing as the welt. You won't be able to see this line of stitching, so keep the zipper foot close to the welt. Leave an opening in the bottom seam for turning.

Step 9: Turn the cushion right side out.

Insert padding and blind-stitch the opening closed (Photo 149).

Step 10: Attach the bra fasteners to the ends of the elastic, and spray the finished pad (Photo 150) with a fabric protector.

150

Bookmark I

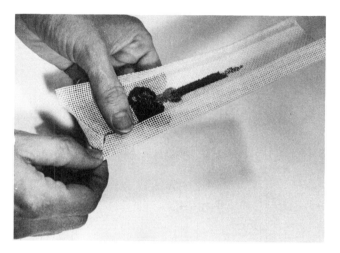

151

152

MATERIALS:
  Ribbon
  Matching thread
  Glue
  Bell

Step 1: Work needlepoint and block.

Step 2: Trim unworked surplus canvas to within ¼ inch of needlepoint on all sides.

Step 3: Fold under surplus canvas and miter corners (Photo 151).

Step 4: Cut ribbon to desired length.

Step 5: Fold one end of the ribbon under ¼ inch and glue in place.

Step 6: Fold the corners of the other end of the ribbon toward the center and glue in place (Photo 152).

Step 7: Position needlepoint on the right side of the prepared ribbon and blind-stitch in place.

Step 8: Sew a small bell at the pointed end of the ribbon (Photo 153).

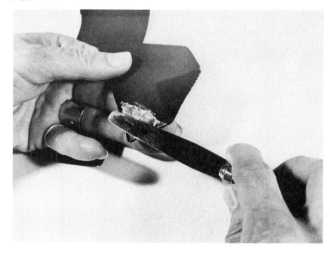

Note: If you have the pointed end of
the ribbon and bell at the top you will
be able to leave the bookmark in place
if the book is standing on a shelf.

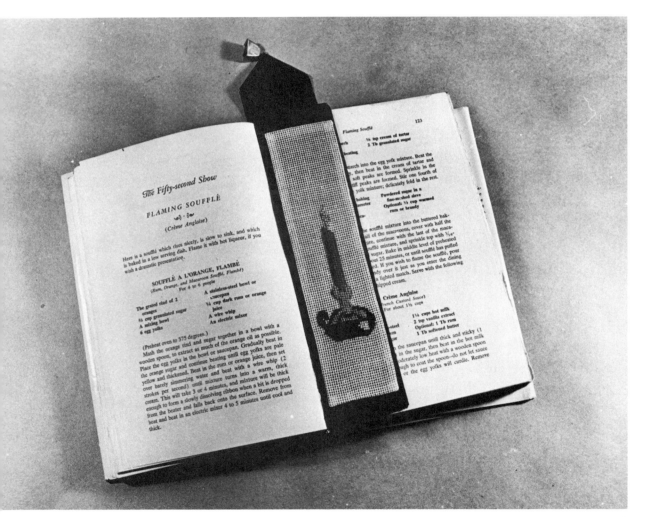

Bookmark II

MATERIALS:
  Ribbon
  Matching thread

Step 1: Work needlepoint and block.

Step 2: Trim unworked surplus canvas to within ¼ inch of needlepoint on all sides.

Step 3: Turn ¼ inch unworked canvas under with the outside rows of needlepoint right on the edges. Steam-press.

Step 4: Fold the top end of the ribbon so the edge of the ribbon is across the end with the diagonal fold on top. Press (Photo 154).

Step 5: Trim the cut end of the ribbon even with the edge.

Step 6: Fold the bottom end of the ribbon as you did the top. Press and trim this end (Photo 154).

Step 7: Position needlepoint on top of the ribbon with the diagonal folds inside.

Step 8: Machine-stitch needlepoint to the ribbon across the top, sides, and bottom.

Step 9: Give the finished bookmark (Photo 155) a final light pressing and spray with a fabric protector.

154

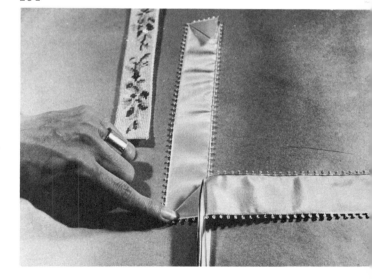

155

Card Table Cover

MATERIALS:
  Non-slip lining fabric
  Seam binding, twill tape, or bias tape
  Decorative edging (optional)
  Curved needle
  Matching or invisible thread

Step 1: Block needlepoint.
Step 2: Trim surplus needlepoint canvas to ½ inch on all edges.
Step 3: Blind-stitch corner seams on right side.

Step 4: Trim corner seams to ¼ inch.
Step 5: Fold the ½ inch of unworked canvas on the bottom to the inside and steam-press in place.
Step 6: Hand-sew seam binding over corner seams and around the bottom edge.
Step 7: Apply decorative edging if you are going to use it (Photo 156).
Step 8: Measure and cut the lining fabric 1 inch larger, on all sides, than the cover.
Step 9: Measure and mark the depth of seam, minus ½-inch seam allowance at each corner of lining fabric (Photo 157).
Step 10: Fold fabric diagonally, matching seams, and machine-stitch corner seams (Photo 158).
Step 11: Center lining over cover, wrong sides together, and pin enough to keep in place.
Step 12: Fold back about 1 foot of lining and sew to within 1 foot of each edge. Use a long running stitch about 1 inch long (Photo 159). Do this on all four sides. This tacking of the lining to the cover will prevent ballooning.

156

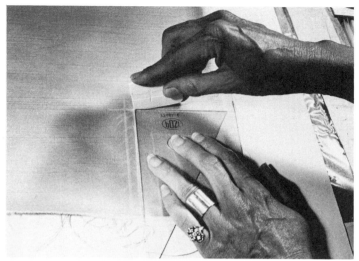

157

158

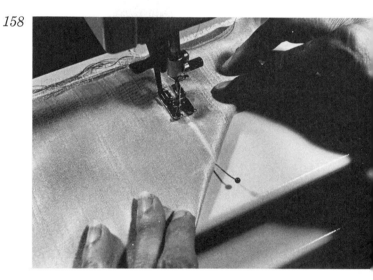

159

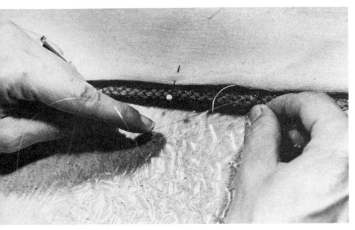

Step 13: Fold under the 1-inch seam allowance on the lining and blind-stitch it to the needlepoint on all edges (Photo 160).

Step 14: Lightly steam the inside edge of the lining and give the outside several light coats of a fabric protector. The finished cover is shown in Photo 161.

160

161

Christmas Tree Ornaments

MATERIALS:
- Lining fabric
- Flannel
- Cardboard
- Padding (either quilt batting, polyfoam, or absorbent cotton)
- Decorative trim for edge
- Glue

Step 1: Trim surplus canvas to within ¼ inch of the blocked needlepoint.

Step 2: Cut a piece of lining to this size.

Step 3: Cut a piece of flannel the same size as the worked area of needlepoint.

Step 4: Cut one piece of cardboard about ⅛ inch smaller than the worked area of needlepoint.

Step 5: Cut one piece of padding ½ inch smaller than the cardboard. Cut another piece of padding the same size as the cardboard. All cut pieces are shown in Photo 162.

Step 6: Put a spot of glue in the center of the cardboard and position the smaller piece of padding in the mid-

162

163

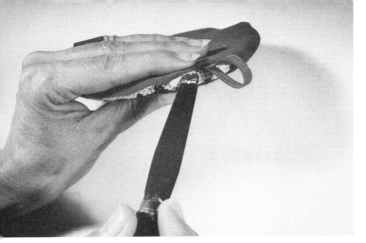

164

165

166

dle. Just a spot of glue on the top and bottom edges will hold the larger piece of padding in place over this.

Step 7: Position needlepoint over the padding and cardboard. Glue the unworked canvas edges to the back of the piece of cardboard. Hold the edges in place with clips or clothespins until dry.

Step 8: Fold a 3-inch piece of trim in half and glue it to the top center of the back (Photo 163).

Step 9: Lay the flannel over the back of the ornament for a lightweight padding.

Step 10: Fold the edge of the lining under only at the point where it covers the tab, and glue the lining in place here. Continue to glue the lining over the edge without turning the lining under. Trim the surplus lining edges close (Photo 164).

Step 11: Glue decorative trim over the raw edges of the lining (Photo 165).

Step 12: Spray with a fabric protector and it is ready to hang (Photo 166).

Note: Ornaments of uneven shapes, like the Christmas tree in Photo 166, are not any more difficult to mount. Just remember you will have to cut the cardboard slightly smaller than you would for an ornament with an even edge.

Desk Blotter—Covered Corners

MATERIALS:

One piece of double-weight mat
board, 22¼ inches by 15¼ inches
One piece of mat board, 8½ inches
by 4¼ inches
One piece of ¼-inch-thick foam
padding, 8½ inches by 4¼ inches
Brown paper, approximately
17 inches by 46 inches
Spray adhesive
Glue

167

Step 1: Measure and mark four triangles on your needlepoint canvas, as
shown in Photo 167. This layout
avoids waste. Allow at least 2 inches
of unworked canvas between diagonal edges and 1 inch between straight
edges of needlepoint. The triangles
should measure 5½ inches on the
straight sides and 7½ inches on the
diagonal. Work the needlepoint and
block.
Step 2: Measure and cut, from the
small piece of mat board, four triangles measuring 4½ inches on the
straight sides with a 6-inch diagonal.

Cut four triangles of foam padding
the same size.
Step 3: Use spray adhesive to glue the
foam padding to the four pieces of
mat board.
Step 4: Cut the needlepoint corners
apart. Place these mat board pieces
on needlepoint with the padding facing the wrong side of the needlework.

Center these pieces on the diagonal sides ¼ inch in from the last row of stitching. Fold over the surplus canvas on this long edge and glue in place with the last row of needlepoint just over the edge (Photo 168). Allow the glue to dry. Cover the remaining padded pieces of mat board the same way.

Step 5: Cut a piece of brown paper large enough to cover one side and fold under all edges of your large piece of mat board. Use spray adhesive to glue this piece of paper to the mat board.

Step 6: Position a padded needlepoint piece on the right side to cover the corner and sides of the board. Fold over the surplus canvas and glue it in place (Photo 169). Clip out the bulk

168

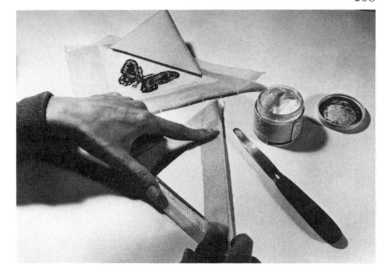

169

surplus canvas at the corner. Repeat for all four corners. Apply pressure to each corner and allow to dry.

Step 7: Cut the remaining piece of brown paper to cover the entire bottom. Use spray adhesive to glue this paper in place, concealing the surplus needlepoint canvas (Photo 170).

Step 8: Spray needlepoint with a fabric protector. Cut a blotter to the correct size and slip it under each corner (Photo 171).

170

171

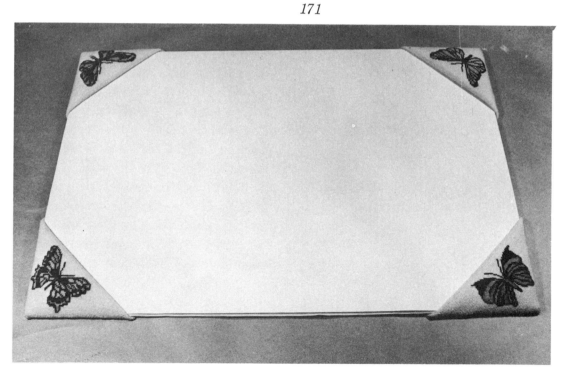

Folding Chair

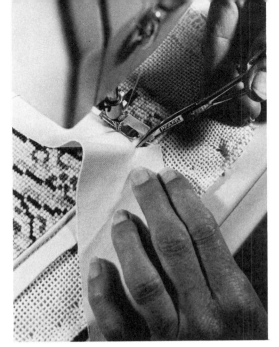

173

MATERIALS:

    1 yard canvas to match canvas on
        chair
    1-inch-thick foam padding to fit seat
    ½-inch-thick foam padding to fit
        back
    Cord for bias welt or purchased welt
    Matching thread
    Zipper foot on your sewing machine

172

Note: You will notice in Photos 172, 173, 174, 175, and 176 that the worked needlepoint area extends beyond the welt for about 1 inch on one side. The reason for this is that the needlepoint was worked too wide for the seat. The thickness of the needlepoint will not fit under the bottom of the arms. The needlepoint was trimmed off to ½ inch, as in Step 12. Needlepoint can be cut—as long as you allow enough seam to prevent raveling. You can also glue or machine-overcast the cut edge.

Step 1: Measure the seat of the chair from back to front and side to side between the bottom of the wooden arm pieces.

Step 2: Measure the piece of canvas for the back from top to bottom and from the line of stitching on one side to the other line of stitching.

Step 3: Work needlepoint pieces to these measurements. Block needle-point.

Step 4: Make a bias welt of canvas to fit around the outside edges of both pieces of needlepoint.

Step 5: Sew the bias welt to the edges of both pieces of needlepoint (Photo 172). Clip corners of welt as you sew.

Step 6: Measure and cut a 2-inch-wide strip of canvas the same length as the bias welt for the box side of the seat. A ½-inch seam is allowed here. If you are using padding thicker than 1 inch you will have to measure the thickness of the padding and add 1 inch for your seam allowance.

Step 7: Measure and cut a 1½-inch-wide strip to fit around the piece of needlepoint for the back.

Step 8: Stitch the 2-inch-wide strip to the edge of the seat, over the welt (Photo 173). Clip at the corners as you sew to make the turn.

Step 9: Continue sewing the strip to each edge of the seat (Photo 174).

Step 10: Sew both ends of the strip together at the end. Trim this seam to ½ inch (Photo 175). Box will look like Photo 176 when you finish sewing.

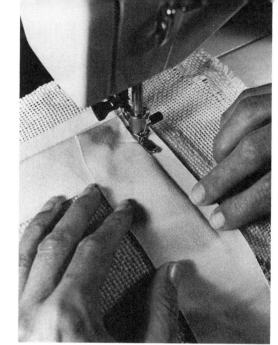

174

175

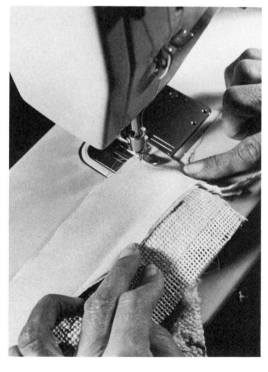

Step 11: Follow Steps 6 through 10, using the 1½-inch-wide strip for the boxed edge of the back of the chair.

Step 12: Trim all seams to ½ inch on both pieces and turn right side out. You now have the top and sides of a boxed cushion.

Step 13: Cut the 1-inch-thick piece of foam padding to fit inside the box for the seat. Place the padding inside the box.

Step 14: Position the box with padding over the canvas seat. Fold under the ½-inch seam allowance and blind-stitch the lower edge of the box to all sides of the seat (Photo 177).

Step 15: Follow Steps 13 and 14, using the ½-inch-thick foam padding for

176

the back of the chair. Position the box on the two lines of stitching on the original back and blind-stitch the box in place.

Step 16: Place seat and back on the chair (Photo 178) and spray both lightly with a fabric protector.

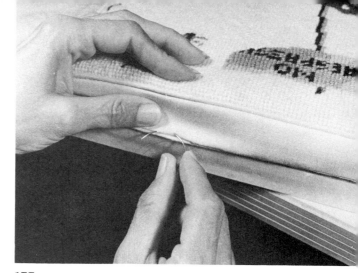

177

178

Padded Picture

MATERIALS:

    Foam core board

    Mat board

    ¼-inch-thick polyfoam padding

    Glue

    Thick fabric for frame

    Thin fabric for back

    Middy braid or narrow tape for hanger

    Pressure boards

    Four "C" clamps

Step 1: Measure the size of the needlepoint after it has been blocked. Trim the unworked canvas to ½ inch.

Step 2: Cut a piece of polyfoam padding ¼ inch smaller than the worked needlepoint area.

Step 3: Cut a piece of core board to the desired frame size.

Step 4: Measure and mark an area the same size as the needlepoint in the center of the core board.

179

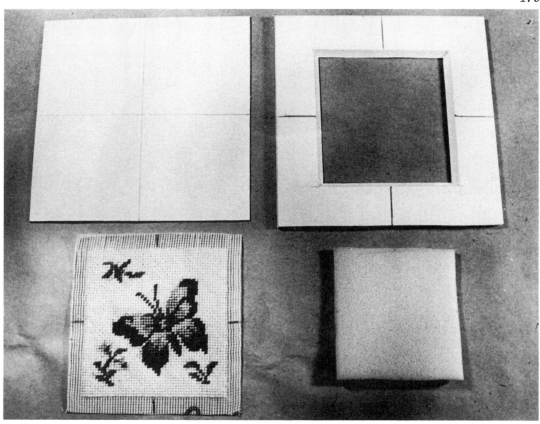

Step 5: Cut this area from the core board. You must cut this line with a beveled edge. If you have difficulty cutting this bevel, have your local picture framer do this for you.

Step 6: Measure and cut a piece of mat board ¼ inch smaller than the core board.

Step 7: Measure and mark, for accurate placement, each piece of core board, mat board, needlepoint, and foam padding, as shown in Photo 179.

Step 8: Center the polyfoam padding on the mat board and glue it in place. You won't need very much glue (Photo 180).

Step 9: Center needlepoint over the polyfoam padding. Glue one edge at a time, on unworked canvas only. Apply pressure to the glued area and allow to dry (Photo 181).

Step 10: Cut the cover fabric for the frame at least 1 inch larger, on all sides, than the core board.

Step 11: Fold the outside edges of the fabric to the back and glue it in place.

Step 12: Clip the surplus fabric from the corners (Photo 182) and glue the corner edge in place.

Step 13: Mark and cut the fabric from the center, leaving ½ inch on all sides.

Step 14: Clip the fabric in the corners right to the edge of the core board.

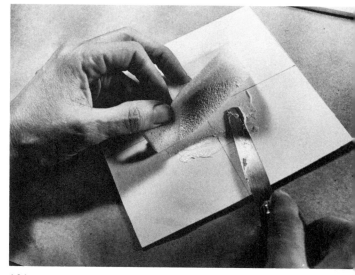

180

181

Step 15: Glue these fabric edges to the back of the core board (Photo 183).

Step 16: Cut a piece of fabric for the back ½ inch larger on all sides than the piece of mat board with the needlepoint attached.

Step 17: Center the mat board over the fabric. Put a touch of glue on each corner of the mat and fold the points over.

Step 18: Fold the straight edges of the fabric over, mitering corners, and glue

182

183

in place one edge at a time. Apply pressure to each edge after gluing (Photo 184).

Step 19: Measure one-fourth of the distance down from the top of the mat and mark it for the placement of the tape for hanging.

Step 20: Stretch the tape at these marks across the back of the mat and glue them in place on the needle-point side (Photo 185).

Step 21: Apply glue to the mat all around the needlepoint. Position this covered piece over the back side of

184

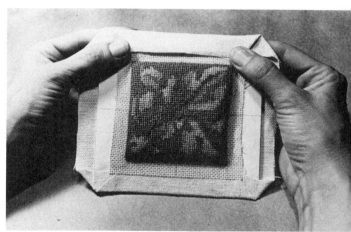

185

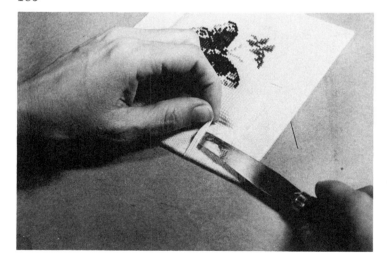

the covered frame and apply pressure (Photo 186). If you have used velveteen for the frame, do not use too much pressure or the velveteen will be crushed.

Step 22: Give the finished frame and needlepoint (Photo 187) a light coat of fabric protector. Vacuum the picture occasionally to keep it clean.

186

187

Picture Frame

MATERIALS:

Fabric for back of frame approximately five times the size of frame

¼-inch-thick polyfoam padding, same size as frame

Mat board or stiff cardboard, four times the size of frame

One file card long enough to fit across bottom of frame

4 or 5 inches of ¼-inch ribbon

Twill tape or heavy fabric, 1 inch wide by 2 inches long

Glass

Spray adhesive

Glue

Note: The exact measurements for fabric, padding, and mat board will depend on the size frame you decide to make. Fabric for covering the various pieces of mat board should be cut with ½-inch allowances on all sides. To cover the pieces of mat board, simply spray one side with adhesive, apply fabric, and roll with a rolling pin for a close bond. Turn the piece over. Spray the edges of the board and finger-press raw edges of fabric in place.

Step 1: Work the needlepoint area a good ¼ inch wider than the desired finished dimensions on all outside edges of the frame. Work needlepoint ⅛ inch beyond the desired finished edge in the center. Block needlepoint and allow to dry.

Step 2: Measure and cut one piece of mat board to the desired finished size of the frame.

Step 3: Measure and cut a piece of foam padding ⅛ inch smaller on all edges than the piece of mat board (Photo 188).

188

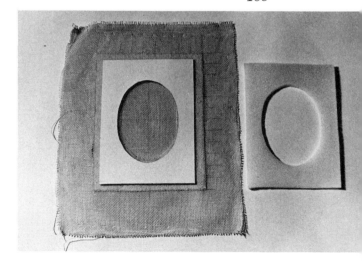

Step 4: Spray one side of the mat board with adhesive, center the padding over it, and press in place.

Step 5: Cut away the surplus unworked canvas in the center of needlework to within 1 inch of the last row of needlepoint. Clip the canvas to the center on a rectangular opening or clip every ½ inch in an oval opening.

Step 6: Center the piece of padded mat board over the back of the needlepoint with the foam side on the needlepoint. Glue the surplus canvas in the opening to the back of the mat board with one row of the needlepoint right on the edge of the board.

Step 7: Cut another piece of mat board ⅛ inch smaller on the outside edges than the previously cut piece. Cut the inside edge ¼ inch in from the center opening edge on the top, bottom, and sides. This piece of mat board will hold the glass in place, so cut a rectangular opening even if the frame opening is oval. Have a piece of glass cut to fit this opening.

Step 8: Glue this piece of mat board to the back of the padded mat board, over the ends of the surplus canvas in the center.

Step 9: Glue the outside edges of the unworked canvas over the last piece of mat board. Miter the corners and clip away as much surplus canvas as

189

possible, to eliminate bulk (Photo 189). Make sure you have the last row of needlepoint over the edge of the mat board. Apply pressure and allow to dry.

Step 10: Cut a piece of file card to cover the bottom side of the frame to within ½ inch of each side. Cover this piece of file card with fabric and glue it to the bottom of the frame (Photo 190).

Step 11: Cut another piece of mat board ⅛ inch smaller on all sides than the finished size of the frame. You are going to use the piece you remove from the middle. The cutting line

190

191

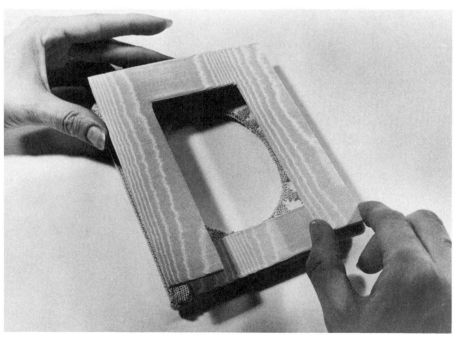

should be ¼ inch deeper on the top and sides than the original opening. Cut the piece you remove from the center ⅛ inch smaller on the top and sides, to allow for a double thickness of fabric. Cover both of these pieces with fabric (Photo 191).

Step 12: Glue the outer, three-sided piece to the back of the frame by applying a ½-inch-wide band of glue around the outside top and side edges. Position the covered board in place and apply pressure. You want just the outside edges of this piece glued, as the glass and easel back have to slip under the inside edges.

Step 13: Use the covered piece removed from the center in Step 11 as a guide. Cut a piece of mat board ¼ inch larger on the top and side edges. Cover this piece with fabric.

Step 14: Measure and cut another piece of mat board for the easel. The dimensions are approximately 1 inch wide at the top, 1½ inches wide at the bottom, and two-thirds the height of the frame. Glue the 1-by-2-inch strip of heavy fabric to extend 1 inch beyond the narrow end of this piece.

Step 15: Cut a piece of fabric large enough to cover the easel and glue it to one side of the mat board and fabric tab (Photo 192). Glue a 4- or 5-inch (depending on the size of the frame) length of ribbon to the bot-

192

tom of the easel. Spray this side of the easel with adhesive and fold the raw edges of fabric in place.

Step 16: Line up the wider end of this piece with the bottom edge of the small piece you have left from Step 11. Mark a cutting line the width of the narrow end for the heavy fabric tab to fit through. Mark another line wide enough for the ribbon to go through, 1 inch from the bottom. Make these slits with a sharp knife or razor blade. Push a ½-inch end of ribbon and the fabric tab through these slits. Glue in place on the back.

Step 17: Glue this piece with the easel to the back side of the piece you made in Step 13 (Photo 193). Apply pressure until dry.

193

Step 18: Lift the lower inner corners of the back of the frame and carefully insert a piece of glass that has been cut to size. Put your picture in place over the glass and then slide the easel back in place under the edges (Photo 194).

Step 19: Spray the front and back of the finished frame (Photo 195) with a fabric protector.

194   195

Speaker Cover

MATERIALS:

Foam core board, ¼ inch thick

Two Velcro fasteners, heavy-duty size

6 inches of ½-inch ribbon or braid

Note: Work only an open design on the canvas. Do not work the background. You can paint the background any desired color. Use acrylic paints with a brush or give the canvas several thin coats of waterproof spray paint before you draw the design on.

Step 1: Measure the area to be covered.

Step 2: Cut a piece of foam board ¼ inch smaller than this measurement.

Step 3: Measure the location and size of the holes for the speakers. Mark these measurements on the foam board.

Step 4: Cut the marked holes in the foam board with either a single-edge razor or a craft knife (Photo 196).

Step 5: Block the needlepoint and trim the surplus unworked needlepoint canvas to 1 inch.

196

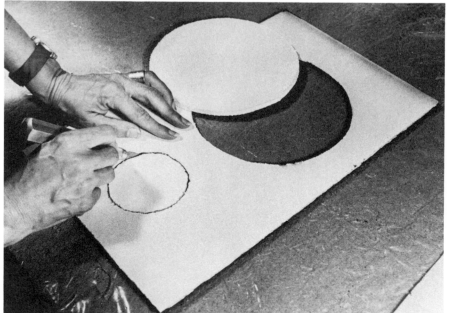

Step 6: Fold the edges of the canvas to the back of the foam board, miter the corners, and either staple or glue the canvas in place. Glue will hold better.

Step 7: Fold a 3-inch piece of ribbon in half to make a tab. Glue the raw ends of this tab over the canvas about ¾ inch down from the back top edge. Center it.

Step 8: Glue or staple one half of a Velcro fastener on top of the raw ends of the tab (Photo 197).

Step 9: Glue one half of another Velcro fastener to the back center bottom edge over the surplus canvas.

Step 10: Glue the remaining halves of the Velcro fasteners to the center top and bottom of the speaker.

Step 11: Spray the right side of the cover with a fabric protector and position in place over the exposed loudspeakers (Photo 198).

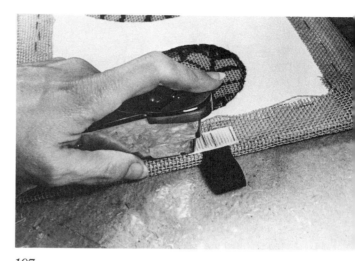

197

198

Tea Cozy

MATERIALS:
  ½ yard velveteen
  Cording or string for welt
  ½ yard quilted fabric
  Matching thread
  Curved needle

Step 1: Measurements of the needle-point should be 11 inches high by 14 inches wide. Round off top corners. This will fit most 6-cup teapots. Work needlepoint and block.

Step 2: Make a bias welt of velveteen to fit up the sides and across the top of the tea cozy.

Step 3: Make another piece of welt to fit all around the bottom, plus 2 inches for overlap.

Step 4: Machine-stitch the welt to the outer sides and top of the needle-point (Photo 199).

Step 5: Trim away the surplus unworked canvas to within ½ inch of the needlepoint on all sides.

199

Step 6: Lay needlepoint over the velveteen and cut velveteen to this size for the back of the tea cozy.

Step 7: Cut a piece of velveteen 4 inches by 6 inches.

Step 8: Fold this piece in half lengthwise, right sides together.

Step 9: Machine-stitch the 6-inch length of this piece.

Step 10: Turn the piece right side out.

Step 11: Insert a 6-inch length of cord along one edge and machine-stitch in place, on the right side, with the zipper foot.

Step 12: Insert another 6-inch length of cord in the other edge and machine-stitch this in place.

Step 13: Fold this piece in half, raw ends together, and pin it at the center top.

Step 14: Sew it in place over the welt.

Step 15: Pin the needlepoint and velveteen right sides together.

Step 16: Use a zipper foot to machine-stitch the two pieces together on the velveteen side (Photo 200).

Step 17: Machine-stitch the remaining piece of welt around the bottom edge of the tea cozy (Photo 201). Start the welt in the center of the velveteen edge. Lap the end of the welt over the start of the welt with a straight line of stitching (Photo 202). Trim ends of welt.

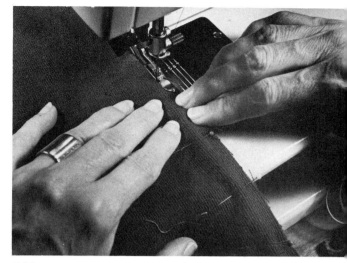

200

201

Step 18: Lay the tea cozy over a double thickness of quilted lining fabric and cut the lining to this size.

Step 19: Machine-stitch the top and sides of the lining fabric, right sides together. The seam allowance should be just a bit deeper than it is on the needlepoint piece.

Step 20: Trim the seam allowance to a little more than ¼ inch (Photo 203).

202

203

Step 21: Steam the bottom raw edge of the tea cozy to the inside toward the top.

Step 22: Fit the lining inside the tea cozy with wrong sides together.

Step 23: Fold the bottom edge of the lining inside and pin in place (Photo 204).

Step 24: Blind-stitch the lining to the bottom edge. The finished tea cozy is shown in Photo 205.

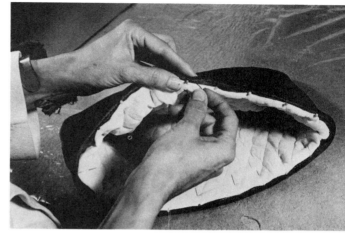

204

205

Yellow Pad Cover

MATERIALS:
    ⅓ or ½ yard lining fabric
    Two pieces of mat board
    Two pieces ¼-inch-thick foam
      padding
    One or two manila file folders
    Glue
    Spray adhesive
    One piece of canvas 4 inches wide by
      length of cover

Note: Exact outside dimensions depend on whether you make a cover for a large or a small pad. The following measurements apply to either size.

Step 1: Work a piece of needlepoint twice the width of your yellow pad, plus 4½ inches wider. The other dimension should be 1½ inches longer than the pad. Block the needlepoint

206

and trim the unworked surplus canvas to within ¾ inch of the last row
of needlepoint.

Step 2: Cut two pieces of mat board
½ inch wider than the pad and ½
inch shorter than the needlepoint
(Photo 206).

Step 3: Cut two pieces of foam padding
the same size as the mat board
(Photo 206).

Step 4: Spray one side of both pieces
of mat board with adhesive and apply the padding.

Step 5: Place these pieces on the
needlepoint with the padding facing
the wrong side of the needlepoint.
Center them top to bottom and ¼
inch in from the side edges. Fold over
the surplus canvas and glue it in
place. Have the last row of needlepoint just over the edge of the mat
board (Photo 207). Apply pressure.

Step 6: Cut the canvas strip the length
of the mat board and glue a ½-inch
edge of its length to one piece of mat
board and the other edge to the second piece of board. The canvas covers
the space between the two pieces of
mat board for reinforcement.

Step 7: Fold the top and bottom edges
of the surplus canvas over the mat
board and canvas strip (Photo 208).
Glue the canvas in place, as in Step

207

208

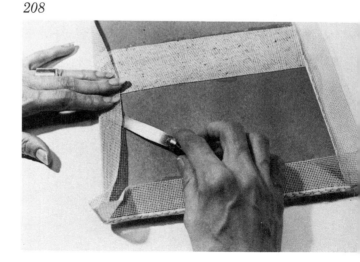

5. Trim the bulk at the corners when dry and reapply glue and clips at the corners if necessary (Photo 209).

Step 8: Cut a piece of lining fabric long enough to cover the canvas strip plus 1 inch. Turn the top and bottom ½ inch under for smooth ends and glue in place with adhesive (Photo 209).

Step 9: Cut two pieces of file folder the same size as the mat board. Cut another strip of file folder the same width as the mat board and 1 inch wide.

Step 10: Cover the two larger pieces of

209

210

file folder with lining fabric, using spray adhesive. Cover the 1-inch strip, allowing 1 extra inch of fabric at each end.

Step 11: Position the covered narrow strip over one large covered piece, 1 inch from the top. Fold the fabric ends to the back and glue in place (Photo 210). This strip will hold the yellow pad in place.

Step 12: Cut another piece of file folder half the length of and the same width as the mat board.

Step 13: Cut a piece of lining fabric large enough to fold over the top and

211

212

cover both sides. Add about 1 inch to turn under on both sides and bottom. Glue this piece of lining fabric on both sides of the folder with spray adhesive.

Step 14: Position this piece over the other large covered piece of file folder. Fold the surplus fabric edges to the bottom and sides and glue them in place (Photo 211).

Step 15: Spread glue all over the back of the lining piece just completed and position it over the mat board inside the cover on the left side. Apply pressure and allow to dry.

Step 16: Glue the other half of the lining to the right inside cover.

Step 17: Fold the cover in half over a large pencil or wooden spoon handle and steam the fold on the outside. Spray the inside with a fabric protector. Slip the back of the yellow pad under the strip near the top on the right side (Photo 212).

Step 18: Spray the needlepoint (Photo 213) with a fabric protector also.

213

Recommended Products

DESCRIPTION AND USE	NAME OR TYPE	WHERE TO BUY IT	MANUFACTURER
Acrylic spray: Spraying canvas to waterproof paints	Tuffilm Krylon Crystal Clear	Art supply stores Art supply stores	M. Grumbacher, Inc. Bordon Chemical Co.
Adhesives: Bonding fabric to fabric, etc.	Tri-Tix Rubber Cream	Mail order	MacMillan Arts & Crafts, 9645 Gerwig Lane, Columbia, Md. 21046
Bonding fabric to mat board	Bond Instant Gr-r-rip Pressure-sensitive spray adhesive	Craft stores Craft and hardware stores	Bond Adhesives Co.
"C" clamps: Applying pressure	Metal "C" clamps	Hardware stores	
Curved needles: Hand sewing	Clark's Home Craft Asst. #H-38	Notions counters	Coats & Clark's
Extra-fine size	Surgical needles, half-circle, taper points	Medical and surgical suppliers	
Drive punch: Making holes in needlepoint	Round drive punch, #3, 9/64"	Mail order	Tandy Leather Co., P.O. Box 2686, Ft. Worth, Texas 76101
Dry cleaners: Removing grease spots	Perchloroethylene, trichloroethane, and trichloroethylene	Drug-, grocery, and hardware stores	
Naphthas	Zippo Lighter Fluid	Drug- and grocery stores	Zippo Mfg. Co.
Combination cleaner	Glamorene Dry Cleaner	Grocery and hardware stores	Glamorene Prod. Corp.

DESCRIPTION AND USE	NAME OR TYPE	WHERE TO BUY IT	MANUFACTURER
Interlinings:			
Lightweight and flexible	Permacrin	Drapery fabric stores	Conso Products
Heavyweight	Permette Cornice Fabric	Drapery fabric stores	Conso Products
Cardboard	Mat board, regular or double weight	Picture framers	
Firm, light foam	Foam core board	Picture framers	
Mat cutter: Beveled-edge and straight cutter	X-Acto "T" Cutter and Beveller #110	Art and craft stores	X-Acto, Inc.
Plastic ruler: Measuring	C-Thru Ruler, 18-inch	Art and craft stores	C-Thru Ruler Co.
Polyfoam: Padding	Polyurethane foam padding	Upholstery supply stores	
Rivets: Securing straps	Extra Long Rivets	Mail order	Tandy Leather Co. P.O. Box 2686, Ft. Worth, Texas 76101
Rivet setter: Securing straps	Rivet Setter #8100	Mail order	Tandy Leather Co. P.O. Box 2686, Ft. Worth, Texas 76101
Stainless-steel pins: Blocking	"T" Blocking Pins Clinton Wig Pins	Knit shops Drugstores	The Boye Needle Co. Scoville Mfg. Co.
Steamers: Blocking and pressing	Oster Steam Wand Today Iron Osrow Steamstress II	Department stores Department stores Department stores	John Oster Mfg. Co. Sunbeam Corp. Osrow Prod. Co.

Needlework Sources

The Artistic Needle, Forest Plaza, Annapolis, Md. 21401—Evening Bag, Tennis Racquet Cover.

Greengage Designs, P.O. Box 9683, Washington, D.C. 20016—Blotter Corners, Bottle Carrier, Folding Chair, Hatband, Pet Bed, Picture Frame, Tobacco Pouches, and Yellow Pad Cover.